BLACK LEGACY PRESS™
WWW.BLACKLEGACYPRESS.ORG

SLAVE NARRATIVES

VOLUME XIV
SOUTH CAROLINA NARRATIVES
PART 4

By
United States.
Work Projects Administration

Copyright © 2024 by BLACKLEGACYPRESS.ORG

All rights reserved. No part of this publication may be reproduced or transmitted in any form or by any means electronic or mechanical, including information storage and retrieval systems without permission in writing from the publisher, except for student research using the appropriate citations.

ISBN: 978-1-63652-203-6

SLAVE NARRATIVES

A Folk History of Slavery in the United States.
From Interviews with Former Slaves

**UNITED STATES.
WORK PROJECTS ADMINISTRATION**

TYPEWRITTEN RECORDS PREPARED BY
THE FEDERAL WRITERS' PROJECT
1936-1938
ASSEMBLED BY
THE LIBRARY OF CONGRESS PROJECT
WORK PROJECTS ADMINISTRATION
FOR THE DISTRICT OF COLUMBIA
SPONSORED BY THE LIBRARY OF
CONGRESS

WASHINGTON 1941

VOLUME XIV

SOUTH CAROLINA NARRATIVES
PART 4

**Prepared by
the Federal Writers' Project of
the Works Progress Administration
for the State of South Carolina**

CONTENTS

Mary Raines 1
Frank Range 5
Sam Rawls 7
Sam Rawls 11
Ellen Renwick 13
Anne Rice 15
Jesse Rice 19
Phillip Rice 25
Martha Richardson 27
Mamie Riley 31
Susie Riser 33
Isom Roberts 35
Alexander Robertson 41
Charlie Robinson 47
Al Rosboro 51
Tom Rosboro 57
Reuben Rosborough 61
William Rose 65
Benjamin Russell 69
Joe Rutherford 73
Lila Rutherford 77
Sabe Rutledge 81
Sabe Rutledge 87

Henry Ryan	93
Henry Ryan	97
Emoline Satterwhite	99
Alexander Scaife	101
Eliza Scantling	103
Mary Scott	107
Nina Scott	117
Morgan Scurry	119
Ransom Simmons	123
Alfred Sligh	125
Dan Smith	129
Hector Smith	135
Hector Smith	139
Hector Smith	141
Hector Smith	143
Hector Smith	145
Jane Smith	147
Mary Smith	151
Mr. Prince Smith	155
Silas Smith	159
Jessie Sparrow	163
Jessie Sparrow	167
Jessie Sparrow	173
Jessie Sparrow	179
Jessie Sparrow	185
Rosa Starke	191

Josephine Stewart	197
Bettie Suber	201
Ellen Swindler	203
Mack Taylor	205
Delia Thompson	209
Robert Toatley	213
Mary Veals	219
Mary Veals	223
Manda Walker	225
Ned Walker	231
Daniel Waring	239
Nancy Washington	243
Charley Watson	247
Dave White	251
Dave White	255
Tena White	259
Bill Williams	263
Jesse Williams	267
Mary Williams	273
Willis Williams	275
Emoline Wilson	281
Emoline Wilson	285
Jane Wilson	287
Genia Woodberry	291
Julia Woodberry	299
Julia Woodberry	305

Julia Woodberry 309
Julia Woodberry 315
George Woods 319
Aleck Woodward 325
Mary Woodward 329
Pauline Worth 333
Daphney Wright 339
Bill Young 343
Bob Young 347

Project #1655
W.W. Dixon
Winnsboro, S.C.

MARY RAINES

Ex-Slave 99 Years Old.

Mary Raines is the oldest living person, white or black, in Fairfield County. If she survives until next December, she will have attained her century of years. She lives with her widowed daughter, Fannie McCollough, fifty-seven years old, and a son, Joe Raines, aged 76 years. They rent a two-room frame house, on lands of Mrs. Sallie Wylie, Chester County, S.C. Joe, the son, is a day laborer on nearby farms. Fannie cooks for Mrs. W.T. Raines. Old Mother Mary has been receiving a county pension of $5.00 per month for several years.

"How old would Marse William Woodward be if he hadn't died befo' I gwine to die? A hundred and twenty, you say? Well, dat's 'bout de way I figured my age. Him was a nephew of Marse Ed, de fust Marse Ed P. Mobley. Him say dat when him 'come twenty-one, old marster give him a birthday dinner and 'vite folks to it. Marse Riley McMaster, from Winnsboro, S.C., was dere a flyin' 'round my young mistress, Miss Harriett. Marse Riley was a young doctor, ridin' 'round wid saddlebags. While they was all settin' down to dinner, de young doctor have to git up in a hurry to go see my mammy. Left his plate piled up wid turkey, nice dressin', rice and gravy, candy 'tatoes, and apple marmalade and cake. De wine 'canter was a settin' on de 'hogany sideboard. All dis him leave to go see mammy, who was a squallin' lak a passle of patarollers (patrollers) was a layin' de lash on her. When de young doctor go and come back, him say as how my mammy done got all right and her have a gal baby. Then him say dat Marse Ed, his uncle, took him to de quarter where mammy was, look me all over and say: 'Ain't her a good one? Must weigh ten pounds. I's gwine to name dis baby for your mama, William. Tell her I name her, Mary, for her, but I 'spects some folks'll call her 'Polly', just lak they call your mama, 'Polly'.

"I was a strong gal, went to de field when I's twelve years old, hoe my acre of cotton, 'long wid de grown ones, and pick my 150 pounds of cotton. As I wasn't scared of de cows, they set me to milkin' and churnin'. Bless God! Dat took me out of de field. House servants 'bove de field servants, them days. If you didn't git better rations and things to eat in de house, it was your own fault, I tells you! You just have to help de chillun to take things and while you doin' dat for them, you take things for yourself. I never call it stealin'. I just call it takin' de jams, de jellies, de biscuits, de butter and de 'lasses dat I have to reach up and steal for them chillun to hide 'way in deir little stomaches, and me, in my big belly.

"When Joe drive de young doctor, Marse Riley, out to see Mass Harriett, while Marse Riley doin' his courtin' in de parlor, Joe was doin' his courtin' in de kitchen. Joe was as smart as de nex' one. Us made faster time than them in de parlor; us beat them to de marriage. Marse Riley call it de altar, but Joe always laugh and say it was de halter. Many is de time I have been home wid them sixteen chillun, when him was a gallavantin' 'round, and I wished I had a got a real halter on dat husband of mine.

"I b'longs to de Gladden's Grove African Methodist 'Piscopal Church. Too old to shout but de great day is comin', when I'll shout and sing to de music of dat harp of 10,000 strings up yonder. Oh! Won't dat be a joyful day, when dese old ailin' bones gonna rise again." (Then the old darkey became suffused in tears, lapsed into a silence and apathy, from which she couldn't be aroused. Finally she slumbered and snored. It would have been unkind to question her further.)

United States. Work Projects Administration

Project 935
Hattie Mobley
Richland County

FRANK RANGE

Civil War Servant And Hero

At the age of one hundred and three, Frank Range is a familiar figure on the streets of Greenville, talking freely of pre-Civil and Civil War days, and the part he played in the war.

Frank, the oldest of nine children, was born of slave parents, Lenard and Elizabeth Herbert, on the plantation of Mr. Jim Boler, Newberry, South Carolina. He was sold several times, and is known by the name of one of his owners, John Range.

During the Civil War his master, Mr. Jim Herbert, carried him to the war as a cook, and when necessary, he was pressed into service, throwing up breast-works; and while he was engaged in this work, at Richmond Va. a terrific bombardment of their lines was made, and a part of their breast-works was crushed in, and his master buried beneath it. Frantic with fear for the safety of his master, Frank began to move the dirt away; finally he was able to drag him to safety. Though shot and shell were falling all around him, he came out unscathed.

Frank Range returned to Newberry at the close of the

war, after which he moved to Greenville County in 1901, and into the city in 1935. He is never happier than when, in the center of a group of willing hearers, he is reciting in a sing-song tone the different periods of his life.

He attributes his longevity to the fact that he has never tasted whiskey, never chewed tobacco; never had a fight; toothache and headache are unknown to him; the service of a physician has never been needed; he does not know one playing card from another. He can walk five or more miles with seeming ease; is jovial and humorous.

He receives a state pension of twenty five dollars annually. His place of residence is 101 Hudson St. Greenville, S.C.

References;

Mr. Guy A. Gullick,
Probate Judge, Greenville County.

Frank Range (information given concerning himself)
101 Hudson St. Greenville S.C.

Project 1885-1
FOLKLORE
Spartanburg Dist. 4
June 15, 1937
Edited by:
Elmer Turnage

SAM RAWLS

Stories From Ex-Slaves

"I was born in 1835 in Lexington County, S.C. I know I was 12 years old de last year of de war. I belonged to John Hiller in Lexington County, near Columbia, S.C. Old Marse Hiller was strict to his slaves, wasn't mean, but often whipped 'em. I thought it was all right then. When de Yankees come through burning, killing and stealing stock, I was in marse's yard. Dey come up whar de boss was standing, told him dere was going to be a battle, grabbed him and hit him. Dey burned his house, stole de stock, and one Yankee stuck his sword to my breast and said fer me to come wid him or he would kill me. O' course I went along. Dey took me as fer as Broad River, on t'other side o' Chapin; then turned me loose and told me to run fast or they would shoot me. I went fast and found my way back home by watching de sun. Dey told me to not go back to dat old man.

"De slaves never learnt to read and write. If any o' dem was caught trying to learn to read or write, dey was whipped bad. I kotched on to what de white chilluns said, and learnt by myself to say de alphabet.

"We went to de white churches atter de war, and set in de gallery. Den de niggers set up a 'brush harbor' church fer demselves. We went to school at de church, and atter school was out in de atternoon, we had preaching.

"Befo' freedom come, de patrollers was strong dere, and whipped any niggers dey kotched out without a pass; wouldn't let dem go to church without a pass.

"Lots of hunting round dere, dey hunted rabbits, squirrels, foxes and 'possums. Dey fished like dey do now.

"De white folks had old brick ovens away from de house, and wide fireplaces in de kitchens. Dey cooked many things on Saturdays, to last several days. Saturday afternoons, we had off to catch up on washing and other things we wanted to do.

"I 'member de Ku Klux and de Red Shirts, but don't 'member anything dey did dere.

"We had corn-shuckings and cotton pickings, when de white people would have everybody to come and help. Us niggers would help. Dey had big suppers afterwards.

"We had plenty to eat from de garden of de boss, a big garden dat furnished all de slaves. Den de boss killed hogs and had other things to eat. Most o' de things raised in de garden, was potatoes, turnips, collards and peas.

"Some of us had witches. One old woman was a witch, and she rode me one night. I couldn't get up one night, had a ketching of my breath and couldn't rise up. She held me down. In dem days, was lots o' fevers with de folks. Dey cured 'em and other sickness wid teas from root herbs and barks.

"Abraham Lincoln was a good man. He said you folks ought to let dem niggers loose and let dem go to work. He come wid his two men, Grant and Sherman, and captured de slave bosses. Jeff Davis was one o' de forerunners of de war. Don't know much about him. Booker T. Washington is a good man. Think he is in office fer a good purpose. I been married four times, Was young man when I married first time. Gussie Gallman, my last wife, is living wid me."

Source: Sam Rawls (84), Newberry, S.C.
Interviewer: G.L. Summer, Newberry, S.C. (6/9/37)

United States. Work Projects Administration

Project 1885-1
Folklore
Spartanburg, Dist. 4
Oct. 13, 1937
Edited by:
Elmer Turnage

SAM RAWLS

Stories From Ex-Slaves

"I live wid my fourth wife and she is much younger dan me. I am unable to work and have to stay in bed lots of de time. My wife works at odd jobs, like washing, ironing and cooking. We rent a two-room house from Miss Ann Ruff.

"I belonged to John Hiller. He was a good master but he worked his slaves hard. Dat was in Lexington County.

"I heard dat Gen. Grant said de slaves ought to get 40 acres of land and a mule so dey could go to work; but dey never got any dat I knows of. Atter Freedom dey worked as wage earners and share-croppers. Some went to other farms to get jobs. Dat's about what dey do now, but some of dem saved a little money and bought farms and some started little businesses of deir own.

"De Ku Klux didn't have much influence wid de slaves or ex-slaves. As soon as de war broke, dey went riding up and down de public roads to catch and beat niggers. My brother run off when dey got atter him. He went to Orangeburg County and stayed down dere.

"I voted twice den, once at Prosperity and again at Newberry. I was a Republican, of course. Some of de Niggers of dis state was elected to office, but dey was not my kinfolks nor special friends. I think niggers ought to vote so dey could vote fer good white folks; and dey ought to run fer office if dey could be elected by good white folks.

"I was sixteen years old when de Yankees come through dis country. Dey caught me in de road and made me go wid dem to Broad River where dey camped one night. Den dey turned me loose and told me to git. I run as fast as I could. I followed de setting sun, de road running towards de sun all de time, and got home about night.

"Since freedom is come de niggers have worked mostly on farms as share-croppers; some as renters wid deir own crops to raise.

"De present generation of niggers ain't got much sense. Dey work when dey want to, and have deir own way about it. De old niggers was learned to work when dey was little.

"I don't know nothing about de Nat Turner Rebellion. I never know'd but one old nigger dat come from Virginia, old Ellen Abner. She lived below Prosperity fer a long time, in de Stoney Hills.

"Yes sir, I tries to live right and git along wid everybody."

Source: Sam Rawls (80), Newberry, S.C.
Interviewer: G.L. Summer, Newberry, S.C. 8/23/37.

Project 1885 -1-
Spartanburg, S.C.
District #4
May 31, 1937
Edited by:
Martha Ritter

ELLEN RENWICK

Ex-Slaves

"I was born on Capt. John P. Kinard's place. My mammy and pa was Lucy and Eph Kinard who belonged to Marse Kinard. Marse Kinard was good to his slaves—didn't whip them much. He whipped me a little. When I was a little girl I slept in the big house in the room with my mistress and her husband, and waited on them. I worked when I got old enough, in the field, and anywhere around. When I wouldn't work good, my mammy whipped me most.

"I 'member the folks cooked in skillets over an old fireplace.

"After the war was over and freedom come we stayed on with Capt. Kinard, 'till I married and then went over to Dock Renwick's place where my husband worked. I married Tom Renwick. We went to the church of the colored folks after the war, and had preachings in mornings and evenings and at night, too. We didn't have no nigger schools, and we didn't learn to read and write.

"The white folks had corn-shuckings, cotton pickings at night, when the mistress would fix a big dinner for all working."

SOURCE: Ellen Renwick (79), RFD, Newberry, S.C.
Interviewer: Mr. G. Leland Summer, 1707 Lindsey St., Newberry, S.C.

Project 1885 -1-
District #4
Spartanburg, S.C.
June 7, 1937

ANNE RICE

Ex-Slaves

"I was born in Spartanburg County, S.C., near Glenn Springs. I can't 'member slavery or de war, but my ma and pa who was Green Foster and his wife, Mary Posey Foster, always said I was a big gal when the war stopped, when freedom come.

"We belonged to Seth Posey who had a big farm there. He was a good man, but sure made us work. I worked in the fields when I was small, hoed and picked cotton, hoed corn. They didn't give us no money for it. All we got was a place to sleep and a little to eat. The big man had a good garden and give us something from it. He raised loads of hogs, to eat and to sell. He sold lots of them. The young fellows hunted rabbits, possums, squirrels, wild turkeys, partridges, doves, and went fishing. The Master's wife, Miss Nancy, was good to us. She had one son, William.

"Yes, I 'member my ma telling us 'bout the padder-rollers. They would ride around, whipping niggers.

"My ma said her step-mother sold her. Sometimes they would take crowds of slaves to Mississippi, taking away mothers from their infant babies, leaving the babies on the floor.

"We always shuck corn and shell it at night, on moonlight nights we pick cotton. On Saturday afternoons we had frolics, sometimes frolics 'till Sunday daylight, then sleep all day Sunday.

"When we got sick all the medicine we took was turpentine—dat would cure almost any ailment. Some of the niggers used Sampson snake weed or peach leaves boiled and tea drunk.

"I joined the church when I was 12 years old 'cause the other girls joined. I think everybody ought to join a church to get their souls right for heaven:

"I married Charley Rice in Spartanburg County, at a colored man's house, named Henry Fox, by a colored preacher named 'Big Eye' Bill Rice. I had four children, and have five grand-children. I have been living in Newberry about 35 years or more. I worked as a wash-woman many years.

"When freedom come, my folks stayed on with Capt. Posey, and I washed and ironed with them later when I was big enough. I done some cooking, too. I could card and spin and make homespun dresses. My ma learned me.

"I don't know much about Abraham Lincoln and Jeff Davis but reckon dey was good men. I never learned to read and write. Booker Washington, I reckon, is a good man."

SOURCE: Anne Rice (75), Newberry, S.C.
Interviewer: G. Leland Summer, 1707 Lindsey St., Newberry, S.C.

United States. Work Projects Administration

Project 1885-1
Folklore
Spartanburg, Dist. 4
Jan. 17, 1937
Edited by:
Elmer Turnage

JESSE RICE

Stories From Ex-Slaves

"My people tells me a lot about when I was a lil' wee boy. I has a clear mind and I allus has had one. My folks did not talk up people's age like folks do dese days. Every place dat I be now, 'specially round dese government folks, first thing dat dey wants to know is your name. Well, dat is quite natu'al, but de very next question is how old you is. I don't know, why it is, but dey sho do dat. As my folks never talked age, it never worried me till jes' here of late. So dey says to me dat last week I give one age to de man, and now I gives another. Soon I see'd dat and I had to rest my mind on dat as well as de mind of de government folks. So I settled it at 80 years old. Dat gives me respect from everybody dat I sees. Den it is de truth, too, kaise I come along wid everybody dat is done gone and died now. De few white folks what I was contemperment (contemporary) wid, 'lows dat I is 80 and dey is dat, too.

"You know dat I does 'member when dat Sherman man went through here wid dem awful mens he had.

Dey 'lowed dat dey was gwine to Charlotte to git back to Columbia. I never is heard of sech befo' or since. We lived at old man Jerry Moss's in Yorkville, way back den. Yes sir, everyone said Yorkville, den, but dey ain't never called Gaffney like dat. Stories goes round 'bout Sherman shooting folks. Some say dat he shot a big rock off'n de State House in Columbia. My Ma and my Pa, Henry and Charity Rice, hid me wid dem when Sherman come along. Us never see'd him, Lawd God no, us never wanted to see him.

"Folks allus crying hard times dese days, ain't no hard times now like it was atter Sherman went through Yorkville. My ma and pa give me ash cake and 'simmon beer to eat for days atter dat. White folks never had no mo', not till a new crop was grow'd. Dat year de seasons was good and gardens done well. Till den us nearly starved and we never had no easy time gitting garden seed to plant, neither.

"Yes sir, if I's handy to locust I makes locust beer; den if I's handy to 'simmons, why den I makes 'simmon beer. Now it's jes' for to pass de time dat us does dat. But gwine back to de war; den it was for necessity. Dese young'uns now don't know what hard times is. Dey all has bread and meat and coffee, no matter how poor dey is. If dey had to live for days and weeks on ash cake and 'simmon beer, as us did den, and work and wait on a crop wid nothing but dat in deir bellies; den dey could grumble hard times. I allus tells 'em to shut up when dey starts anything like dat around me.

"When dat crop come along, we sho did fall in and save all us could for de next year. Every kind of seed and pod dat grow'd we saved and dried for next spring or fall planting. Atter folks is once had deir belly aching and growling for victuals, dey ain't never gwine to throw no rations and things away no mo'. Young folks is powerful wasteful, but if something come along to break up deir good time like it did to us when dat man Sherman held everything up, dey sho will take heed, and dey won't grumble 'bout it neither, cause dey won't have no time to grumble.

"Things passes over quicker sometimes dan we figures out dat dey will. Everything, no matter how good it be or how hard, passes over. Dey jes' does like dat. So dem Yankees went on somewhars, I never know'd whar, and everything round Yorkville was powerful relieved. Den de Confederate soldiers started coming across Broad River. Befo' dey got home, word had done got round dat our folks had surrendered; but dem Yankees never fit (fought) us out—dey starved us out. If things had been equal us would a-been fighting dem till dis day, dat us sho would. I can still see dem soldiers of ours coming across Broad River, all dirty, filthy, and lousy. Dey was most starved, and so poor and lanky. And deir hosses was in de same fix. Men and hosses had know'd plenty till dat Sherman come along, but most of dem never know'd plenty no more. De men got over it better dan de hosses. Women folks cared for de men. Dey brewed tea from sage leaves, sassafras root and other herb teas. Nobody never had no money to fetch no medicine from de towns wid, so dey made liniments and salves from de things dat grow'd around about in de woods and gardens.

"I told you 'bout how small I was, but my brother, Jim Rice, went to Charleston and helped to make dem breastworks down dar. I has never see'd dem, but dem dat has says dat dey is still standing in good conditions. Cose de Yankees tore up all dat dey could when dey got dar.

"Lots of rail fences was made back in dem days. Folks had a 'no fence' law, dat meant dat everybody fenced in deir fields and let de stock run free. Hogs got wild and turkeys was already wild. Sometimes bulls had to be shot to keep dem from tearing up everything. But folks never fenced in no pasture den. Dey put a rail fence all around de fields, and in dem days de fields was never bigger dan ten or fifteen acres. Logs was plentiful, and some niggers, called 'rail splitters', never done nothing else but split rails to make fences.

"If I recollects right, Wade Hampton broke down fence laws in dis country. I sho heard him talk in Yorkville. Dey writ about him in de Yorkville Inquirer and dey still has dat paper over dar till now. De Red Shirts come along and got Wade Hampton in. He scared de Yankees and Carpetbaggers and all sech folks as dem away from our country. Dey went back whar dey come from, I reckon.

"De Ku Klux was de terriblest folks dat ever crossed my path. Who dey was I ain't never know'd, but dey took Alex Leech to Black's Ford on Bullet Creek and killed him for being a radical. It was three weeks befo' his folks got hold of his body.

"Dr. Bell's calves got out and did not come back for a long time. Mrs. Bell fear'd dat dey was gitting wild, so she sent de milk girl down on de creek to git dem calves. Dat girl had a time, but she found 'em and drove 'em back to de lot. De calves give her a big chase and jumped de creek near a big raft of logs dat had done washed up from freshets. All over dem logs she saw possums, musrats and buzzards a-setting around. She took her stick and drove dem all away, wid dem buzzards puking at her. When dey had left, she see'd uncle Alex laying up dar half e't up by all dem varmints.

"She know'd dat it must be him. When she left, dem buzzards went back to deir perch. First thing dey done was to lap up deir own puke befo' dey started on uncle Alex again. Yes sir, dat's de way turkey buzzards does. Dey pukes on folks to keep dem away, and you can't go near kaise it be's so nasty; but dem buzzards don't waste nothing. Little young buzzards looks like down till dey gits over three days old. You can go to a buzzard roost and see for yourself, but you sho better stay out'n de way of de old buzzard's puke. Dey sets around de little ones and keeps everything off by puking.

"Pacolet used to be called Buzzard Roost, kaise in de old days dey had a rail outside de bar-room dat de drunks used to hang over and puke in a gully. De buzzards would stay in dat gully and lap up dem drunkards' puke. One night a old man went in a drunkard's sleep in de bar-room. De bar tender shoved him out when he got ready to close, and he rolled up against dis here rail dat I am telling you about. He 'lowed dat next morning when he woke up, two buzzards was setting on his shirt front eating up his puke. He said, 'You is too soon', and grabbed one by de leg and wrung his head off. But befo' he could git its head wrung off it had done puked his own puke back on him. He said dat was de nastiest thing he ever got into, and dat he never drunk no more liquor. Dem days is done past and gone, and it ain't nobody hardly knows Pacolet used to be called Buzzard Roost.

"Lawd have mercy, white folks! Here I is done drapped

plumb off'n my subject; but a old man's mind will jes' run waa'ry at times. Me and Joe, Alex's son, went to see de officer 'bout gitting Joe's pa buried. He 'lowed dat Alex's body was riddled wid bullets; so we took him and put his bones and a little rotten flesh dat dem buzzards had left, in de box we made, and fetched it to de site and buried him. Nobody ever seed Alex but me, Joe, and dat gal dat went atter dem calves. Us took shovels and throw'd his bones in de box. When we got de top nailed on, we was both sick. Now, things like dat don't come to pass. I still thinks of de awful days and creeps runs all over me yet.

"All my brothers, sisters, mother and father is done gone. And I is looking to leave befo' a great while. I is trying every day to git ready, Lawd. I been making ready for years. Smart mens tries to make you live on, but dey can't git above death. Tain't no use."

Source: Jesse Rice (80), Littlejohn St., Gaffney, S.C.
Interviewer: Caldwell Sims, Union, S.C. 1/8/38

Project 1885-1
FOLKLORE
Spartanburg Dist. 4
June 15, 1937

Edited by:
Elmer Turnage

PHILLIP RICE

Stories From Ex-Slaves

"I'm living on Mr. Russel Emmitt's place. I never did nothing but drive cows when I was a little boy growing up. Miss Cum and Miss Lizzie Rice was Marse Alex's sisters. Marse Alex done died, and dey was my mistress. Dey tuck and sold de plantation afo dey died, here 'bout twenty years ago. Dat whar my ma found me and den she died.

"My grandparents, Jane and Peter Stevens, brung me up. I was a little farm boy and driv cows fer de overseer, Jim Blalock. Miss Cum was really Miss Ann. Miss Ann had a hundred niggers, herself, and Miss Lizzie had might nigh dat many, asides dem what Marse Alex done left 'em. De overseer try to act rough out o' Miss Ann's sight, and she find it out and set him down a peg.

"Miss Jane have our shirts made on de looms. She let us wear long shirts and go in our shirt tails, and us had to keep 'em clean, too, 'cause Miss Jane never like no dirt around her. Miss Jane have charge of de whole house and everything along wid it.

"Us had three hundred hogs to tend to, two hundred yellings and heifers, and Lawdy knows how many sheep and goats. Us fed dem things and kept 'em fat. When butchering time come, us stewed out the mostest lard and we had enough side-meat to supply the plantation the year round. Our wheat land was fertilized wid load after load of cotton seed. De wheat us raised was de talk of de country side. 'Sides dat, dare was rye, oats and barley, and I ain't said nothing 'bout de bottom corn dat laid in de cribs from year to year.

"Our smokehouse was allus full o' things to eat, not only fer de white folks but fer de darkies as well. And our barns carried feed fer de cattle from harvest to harvest.

"De fattest of all de hosses, was Miss Ann's black saddle hoss called, 'Beauty'. Miss Ann wo' de longest side-saddle dress dat hung way down below her feets. Somebody allus had to help her on and off Beauty, but n'ary one of her brothers could out-ride Miss Ann."

Source: Phillip Rice (75), Kelton, S.C. RFD
Interviewed by: Caldwell Sims, Union, S.C. (5/7/37)

Project #1655
Stiles M. Scruggs
Columbia, S.C.

MARTHA RICHARDSON

The Pot Of Gold.

Martha Richardson, who tells this story, lives at 924 Senate Street, Columbia, S.C. Her father was an Indian and her mother a mulatto. She was born in Columbia in 1860 and was five years old, when General W.T. Sherman's Federal troops captured and burned the city in 1865.

"When I gits big 'nough to pick up chips for de cook stove, we was livin' in de rear of Daniel Gardner's home, on Main Street, and my mammy was workin' as one of de cooks at de Columbia Hotel. De hotel was run by Master Lowrance, where de Lorick & Lowrance store is now.

"My daddy, like de general run of Indians, love to hunt but de game not bring much cash in. My mammy often give him some change (money) and he not work much but he always good to mammy and she love him and not fuss at him, much. I soon learn dat if it had not been for mammy, we wouldn't a had much to eat and wear. We go 'long lak dat for a good while and my mammy have friends 'nough dat she seldom had to ask for a job.

"De game was so scarce dat my daddy sometimes

make a little money a showin' people how to make Indian medicine, dat was good for many complaints, how to cover deir houses, and how to kill deir hogs, 'cordin' to de moon. He tell us many times 'bout de great Catawba Indians, who make all deir own medicines and kill bears and dress in deir skins, after feastin' on deir flesh. He was a good talker.

"You know, I sees so much 'skimpin', to make ends meet at home, as we go 'long dis way, dat I has never married. My mammy tell me: 'Honey, you a pretty child. You grow up and marry a fine, lovin' man lak your daddy, and be happy.' I kinda smile but I thinks a lot. If my daddy had worked and saved lak my mammy, we would be 'way head of what we is, and my brudders say so, too. But we fond of our daddy, he so good lookin' and all.

"What de most 'citin' thing I ever see? Well, I think de Red Shirt campaign was. You never see so much talkin', fightin', and fussin' as dat. You know de Yankees was still here and they not 'fraid, and de Hampton folks was not 'fraid, so it was a case of knock down and drag out most of de time, it seem to me. Long at de end, dere was two governors; one was in de Wallace House and one in de Capitol. Men went 'bout town wid deir guns.

"Mammy keep busy cookin', nussin', and washin', and us chillun help. You know I had two brudders older than me and a little baby brudder 'bout a year old, when my mammy rent a small farm from Master Greenfield, down at de end of Calhoun Street, near de Broad River. We plant cotton. I was then eleven years old and my brudder was twelve and thirteen. My mammy help us plant it befo' she go to work at de hotel.

"She was home washin', one day, when my brudders and me was choppin' cotton. We chop 'til 'bout eleven o'clock dat mornin' and we say: 'When we gits out de rows to de big oak tree we'll sit down and rest.' We chillun lak each other and we joke and work fast 'til we comes to de end of de rows and in de shade of de big oak. Then we sets down, dat is, my oldest brudder and me, 'cause my young brudder was a little behind us in his choppin'. As he near de finish, his hoe hit somethin' hard and it ring. Ha rake de dirt 'way and keep diggin', light lak.

"What you doin', brudder?' I say. He say: 'Tryin' to find out what dis is. It seem to be a pot lid.' Then we jump up and go to him and all of us grabble dirt 'way and sho' 'nough it was a pot lid and it was on a pot. We digs it out, thinkin' it would be a good thing to take home. It was so heavy, it take us all to lift it out.

"It was no sooner out than we takes off de lid and we is sho' s'prised at what we see. Big silver dollars lay all over de top. We takes two of them and drops them together and they ring just lak we hear them ring on de counters. Then we grabble in de pot for more. De silver went down 'bout two inches deep. Twenty dollar gold pieces run down 'bout four inches or so and de whole bottom was full of big bundles of twenty dollar greenbacks.

"We walks up to de house feelin' pretty big and my oldest brudder was singin'":

'Hawk and buzzard went to law,
Hawk come back wid a broken jaw.'

"Mammy say widout lookin' at us: 'What you all comin' to dinner so soon for?' Then she looked up and see de pot and say: 'Land sakes, what you all got?' Then we puts de big pot down in de middle of de floor and takes off de lid, and mammy say: 'Oh! Let's see what we has!' She begin to empty de pot and to count de money. She tell us to watch de door and see dat nobody got in, 'cause she not at home!

"She say de money 'mount to $5,700, and she swear us not to say nothin' 'bout findin' it. She would see what she could find out 'bout it. Weeks after dat, she tell us a big white friend tell her he hear a friend of his buried some money and went to war widout tellin' anybody where it was. Maybe he was killed and dat all we ever hear.

"My mammy kept it and we all work on just de same and she buy these two lots on Senate Street. She build de two-story house here at 924, where you sittin' now, and de cottage nex' door. She always had rent money comin' in ever since. By and by she die, after my Indian pappy go 'way and never come back. Then all de chillun die, 'ceptin' me.

"I am so happy dat I is able to spend my old days in a sort of ease, after strugglin' most of my young life and gittin' no learnin' at school, dat I sometimes sing my mammy's old song, runnin' somethin' lak dis:

> 'Possum up de simmon tree
> Sparrow on de ground
> 'Possum throw de 'simmons down
> Sparrow shake them 'round'."

Project#-1655
Phoebe Faucette
Hampton County

Approx. 416 words

MAMIE RILEY
Ex-Slave

"Aunt Mamie's" hair is entirely white. She lives in a neat duplex brick house with one of her husband's relatives, a younger woman who is a cook for a well established family in Estill, S.C. When questioned about the times before the war, she replied:

"Yes'm, I kin tell you 'bout slav'ry time, 'cause I is one myself. I don' remember how old I is. But I remember when de Yankees come through I bin 'bout so high. (She put her hand out about 3½ feet from the floor.) We lived on Mr. Henry Solomons' place—a big place. Mr. Henry Solomons had a plenty of people—three rows of house, or four.

"When de Yankees come through Mr. Solomons' place I wuz right dere. We wuz at our house in de street. I see it all. My ma tell me to run; but I ain't think they'd hurt me. I see 'em come down de street—all of 'em on horses. Oo—h, dey wuz a heap of 'em! I couldn't count 'em. My daddy run to de woods—he an' de other men.

Dey ran right to de graveyard. Too mucha bush been dere. You couldn't see 'em. Stay in de woods three days.

"Dey went to my daddy's house an' take all. My daddy ran. My mother an' my older sister wuz dere. My ma grab a quilt off de bed an' cover herself all over wid it—head an' all. And set in a chair dere by de fire. She tell us to git in de bed—but I ain't git in. And she yell out when she hear 'em comin': 'Dere's de fever in heah!' Six of 'em come to de door; but dey say dey ain't goin' in—dey'll catch de fever. Den some more come along. Dey say dey gwine in. Dey ain't gwine to take no fever. Fill two sack of 'tatoes. White man ask to search all trunk. Dey take two of me Ma's good dresses out. Say to wrap 'tatoes in. I start to cryin' den, an' dey say, 'Well, git us some sacks den.' I knowed where some sacks wuz. I git 'em de sacks. Dey do 'em right. Dey bid 'em goodbye, an' ax 'em where de man wuz. Dey give me 'leven or twelve dollars. I wuz little an' ain't know. My mother never give it to me.

"I stay right on dere after freedom, until after I married."

Source: Mamie Riley, Negro about 80 years old, Estill, S.C.

Project 1885-1
FOLKLORE
Spartanburg Dist. 4
May 24, 1937

Edited by:
Elmer Turnage

SUSIE RISER

Stories From Ex-Slaves

"I was born near Broad River in de Dutch Fork of Newberry County. I was a slave of Cage Suber. He was a fair master, but nothing to brag about. I was small at slavery time and had to work in de white folks' house or around the house until I was big enough to go to de field and work.

"Old Marse Cage always made me fan flies off of him when he lay down to take a nap. The fan was made out of brushes.

"De white folks had cotton-pickings, corn-shuckings and quiltings. Dey allus had something to eat at the frolics and I had to help wid 'em.

"I married John Riser. I moved to town several years ago."

Source: Susie Riser (80), Newberry, S.C.

United States. Work Projects Administration

Interviewer: G.L. Summer, Newberry, S.C., May 17, 1937.

Project #1655
Henry Grant,
Columbia, S.C.

ISOM ROBERTS

Ex-Slave 80 Years Old

Isom Roberts rents one room at 1226 Waverly Street, Columbia, S.C., and lives alone. However frail he appears, he is able to support himself by working in the yards about the city.

"Well, sir, white folks, I is eighty years old, or leastwise I is so close to it, dat it don't make much difference. But even if I is dat old, it don't seem so long since I was a little boy. Years flies by mighty fas' to old folks, 'cause deir 'memberance is shorter, while young folks 'members everything, and in dat way months and years drags 'long slower to them.

"I was a very small boy when de Civil War was gwine on. It seems like I knows all 'bout Sherman's army comin' through dis State, a burnin' Columbia and destroyin' and takin' away everything what folks had. I has heard so much 'bout slavery and all them times, from my mammy and daddy, dat it 'pears to me dat I 'sperienced it all. I 'spects knowin' 'bout things is just 'bout as good and true as seein' them. Don't you?

"My daddy and mammy b'long to Marster Sam Louie,

who had a big plantation over in Calhoun County. He had 'bout fifty or more grown slaves, 'sides many chillun of de slaves. Old marster was a good farmer; raised big crops and saved what he made. He sho' was a fine business man but he was mighty hard on everybody he had anything to do wid. He told his slaves to work hard and make him a heap of money and that he would keep it, in case of hard times. Times was all de time hard wid old marster but de niggers never got no money. When news spread 'round dat de Yankees was comin' to free de niggers, he called all de slaves up in de yard and showed them a big sack of money, what they had made for him, and told them dat he was gwine to kill all of them befo' de Yankees set them free and that they wouldn't need no money after they was done dead. All de slaves was mighty sad and troubled, all dat day, when old marster made dat speech to them. But somethin' happened. It most makes me tremble to talk to you 'bout it now. Providence, or some kind of mercy spirit, was sho' walkin' 'round dat plantation dat night. Sometime in de night it was whispered 'round amongst de slaves dat old marster done took de smallpoxes and was mighty sick. Mammy said he must have been terrible sick, 'cause they buried him two days after dat.

"After old marster flew away, everything was different on de plantation. Miss Nancy, dat was old marster's wife, told de slaves dat when de Yankees freed them, they could stay right there and work on shares or by the day, which ever way they wanted. Many stayed on de plantation after freedom while others went away. Me and my folks stayed on wid Miss Nancy until she die. Then us moved on another plantation in de lower side of de county. I stayed dere until my wife died, seventeen years ago.

"Does I 'member anything 'bout how de slaves was treated in slavery time? Well, I 'members a little myself and a heap of what others told me. Wid dis I has done told you, I believes I want to stop right dere. A low fence is easier to git over than a high one. Say little and you ain't gwine to have a heap to 'splain hereafter. Dere is a plenty of persons dat has lost deir heads by not lettin' deir tongues rest. Marster Sam Louie is dead now. He can't disturb nobody in his grave. He had his faults and done many things wrong but show me dat person what don't mis-step sometimes. All of us, both white and black, is prone to step aside now and then. To tell de truth, old marster never knowed what Sunday was. Everybody on de plantation worked on dat day as same as any other day.

"But Boss, if my old marster was rough and hard and break de Sabbath and all dat, he was no worser than what young white folks and niggers is dese days. You can see them any time, floppin' 'bout in dese automobiles, a drinkin' and a carryin' on. Sich stuff is abomination in de sight of a decent person, much less dat One up yonder. (He pointed upward).

"I's gwine to tell you boss, dat slavery time was better for de average nigger than what they is gittin' now. Folks say dat slavery was wrong and I 'spose it was, but to be poor like a heap of niggers is now, is de worse thing dat has ever come upon them, I thinks. Dis gittin' something wrong, ain't right. De North had no business sellin' niggers to de South and de South had no business buyin' them from de North and makin' slaves of them. Everything went on pretty nice for awhile, then de North got jealous of de South and de South got 'spicious of de North. I believes dat if you can't go over and you can't go under, then you should try to go 'round. If de big men up North and here in de South had been good 'nough and smart 'nough, they might could a gone 'round dat terrible Civil War. I believes dat.

"I marry Lucy Nelson when I was 'bout thirty years old. She was a bright skin nigger, much brighter than I is. She was high tempered and high spirited, too. She was sho' smart, and de best cook I has ever seen. Just plain corn bread, dat she cooked in de hot ashes of de fireplace, taste sweeter and better than de cake you buy now. But de least thing would git her temper 'roused. I has knowed her to complain wid de old hound dog us had, 'cause he didn't run some rabbits out de woods for me to shoot. Fuss wid de cats, 'cause they didn't ketch de mouses in de house. Quarrel wid de hens, 'cause they eat, cackled, scratched and wallowed holes in de yard and wouldn't lay. Told de old rooster many times dat she was gwine to chop his head off if he didn't crow sooner and louder of mornin's and wake me up so I could go to work. All dis sounds foolish I knows but you see how bent my back is. Well, I 'spects it was bent from totin' so many buckets of water from de spring for her to wash wid soon of mornin's, so I could then do a day's work.

"My wife thought she was doin' right by workin' like she did. She thought dat she was helpin' me make a livin' for our big family of eight chillun. Yes sir, I knows now she was right, but hard work broke her health and brought her to her bed where she lingered 'bout one year and then she went away from me. All dis took place seventeen years ago and, from then to dis, I ain't seen no woman I would have for a wife, 'cause I ain't gwine to find no woman Lucy's equal. All my chillun are dead, 'cept two, and I don't know where they is.

"Does poor folks have any blessings and pleasure? Well, yes sir, in a way. You see they don't have no worriments over what they has, like rich folks. They can sleep as hot as they want to in de summer time and raise as big families as anybody. Sho', poor folks, and especially niggers, has a good time on hog-killin' days. In early summer come them juicy brierberries dat they enjoy so much. They last until watermelon season. Then they has 'possum and 'tators in de fall. Most all livin' beings has deir own way of doin' things and deir way of existin'. De hog roots for his, de squirrel climbs for his, de chickens scratches for deirs, and de nigger, well, if dere ain't nobody lookin', I reckon they could slip deirs right handy.

"I sho' has enjoyed talkin' to you dis evening and now, if you will 'scuse me, I's gwine home and cook me a pot of turnips. I can almost taste them now, I is so hungry."

United States. Work Projects Administration

Project #1655
W.W. Dixon
Winnsboro, S.C.

ALEXANDER ROBERTSON

Ex-Slave 84 Years Old.

Alexander Robertson lives as a member of the household of his son, Charley, on the General Bratton plantation, four miles southeast of White Oak, S.C. It is a box-like house, chimney in the center, four rooms, a porch in front and morning glory vines, in bloom at this season, climbing around the sides and supports. Does Alexander sit here in the autumn sunshine and while the hours away? Nay, in fact he is still one of the active, working members of the family, ever in the fields with his grandchildren, poke around his neck, extracting fleecy cotton from the bolls and putting it deftly into the poke. He can carry his row equally as well as any of the six grandchildren. He has a good appetite at meal time, digestive organs good, sleeps well, and is the early riser in the mornings. He says the Negro half of his nature objects to working on Saturday afternoon, and at such times his tall figure, with a green patch cloth over the left eye, which is sightless, may be seen strolling to and fro on the streets of Winnsboro.

"Well, well! If it ain't de youngun dat use to sell me

sugar, coffee, fat back and meal, when he clerk for Calvin Brice & Company, at Woodward, in '84 and 'long dere.

"I hopes you is well dis mornin'. I's told to come to Winnsboro and gits blanks for a pension. Andy Foster, man I knows, d'rect me up dese steps and bless God I finds you. You wanna ask me some questions? Well, here I is, more than glad to answer, if I can. Where I born? Strange as it seems, I born right here in Winnsboro. My name set down in a book: 'Alexander-boy-mother, Hannah, wench of James Stewart'. Dat de way it was read to me by Dr. Beaty, dat marry a Miss Cherry and live in Rock Hill. If slavery had never been done 'way wid, dat would be my master today, 'cause him lak hound dogs and I lak a hound dog. Dat kind of breed got a good nose and make good 'possum dog. Marster Jim tell me one time, dat de first dog sprung from a wolf, and dat fust dog was a hound dog. Dat out dat fust dog, (must to a been a bitch, don't you reckon?) come all dogs. I follow his talk wid belief, 'bout de setters, pointers, and blood hounds, even to de fices, but it strain dat belief when it git to de little useless hairy pup de ladies lead 'round wid a silver collar and a shiney chain. Well, you don't care to hear anymore 'bout dat? What is de question?

"My master at de fust, was Marster Jim Stewart and my mistress was his wife, Mistress Clara. They have two chillun. I 'member Marster Jim and Miss Lizzie; they live in a fine house befo' de war, 'round yonder close to Mt. Zion College. My mother was de cook and I was de house boy. They had a big plantation 'bout two miles out, sorta southwest of Boro, I mean Winnsboro, of course, but de country people still call it Boro.

"On dat plantation was many two-room houses,

brick chimneys in de middle, for de plantation slaves. In de growin' season I go wid marster every day, not to drive, too small for dat, just to hold de hoss, when him git out and then I run errands for him, 'round de house and in de fields.

"My mother had another child, Willie Finch. A colored man name of Finch is his father but her and de white folks never tell me who my father was. I have to find out dat for myself, after freedom, when I was lookin' 'round for a name. From all I hear and 'pear in de lookin' glass, I see I was half white for sure, and from de things I hear, I conclude I was a Robertson which have never been denied. Maybe it best just to give no front names. Though half a nigger, I have tried to live up to dat name, never took it in dat court house over yonder, never took it in dat jail or dat calaboose. I's paid my debts dollar for dollar and owe no man nothin' but good will.

"What de Yankees do when they come? Let other people tell dat, but seem lak they lay de whole town in ashes, 'cept de college and our house close to it, dat they use for de officers while they was in Boro. Why they hear sumpin' bout de Davis name techin' de St. John 'Piscopal Church and they march 'round dere, one cold February Sunday mornin', set it afire, and burn it up. Mother and me went to de plantation and stayed dere 'til they left.

"When freedom come, I was twelve years old. Mother marry a Finch; Bill was de name of him. Our nex' move was to Dr. Madden's place, just north of Boro. Us farm up dere and I do de hoein'. I live dere thirteen years. I got to feelin' my oats and tired of workin' for a plum black nigger, I did. Maybe I ought to been more humble but I wasn't.

"I ask myself one night: 'What you gonna do, stay here forever for your vittles and clothes?' Then come over my mind I old 'nough for to marry. Who I gwine to marry? It pop right in dis head, Sarah was de gal for me. I rode old Beck down dere de nex' Sunday; dat was in December. I come right to de point wid her and de old folks. They 'low they have no objections if I could take care of her. I say I try to. They say: 'Dat ain't 'nough, 'range yourself for another year and then come and git her'.

"De Lord directs me. I's down here payin' my poll, too. Marster Tom Shanty Brice come in as us come out. I ask him if he need a hand for nex' year. He look me up from top to bottom and say: 'What's your name?' I show him my tax receipt. He hire me than and dere. I go right straight to Sarah and us tell de old folks. Rev. Gordon marry us de 29th of January, 1879. Us has seven chillun. Alex, dat's de one name for me, is in Tampa, Florida. Carrie marry a Coleman and is in Charlotte, N.C. Jimmie is dead. Thomas is in Charleston, S.C. Emma marry a Belton and lives wid her husband in Ridgeway, S.C. I stay wid my son, Charley, up de country.

"I voted one time in 1876, for Gov. Chamberlain, but when I moved to Marster Tom Brice's I thought so much of him, I just quit voting. I would lak to vote one more time to say: 'I have vote one time wid de black part of my nature, dis time I votes wid de white side of my nature.' What you laughin' 'bout? If it was de call of dark blood de fust time, maybe it's de call of de white blood dis time. You have no idea de worry and de pain a mulatto have to carry all his eighty-four years. Forced to 'sociate wid one side, proud to be related to de other side. Neither side lak de color of your skin. I jine de Methodist church here in

Boro and 'tend often as I can and as I hear my preacher Owens preach, dat dere will be no sex in hebben, I hopes and prays dat dere'll be no sich thing as a color line in hebben.

"Who de best white men I ever know? Mr. Tom Brice, Mr. W.L. Rosborough, Mr. Watt Sinonton, and Mr. August Nicholson. Master Bill Beaty, dat marry my young mistress, Elizabeth, was a fine man.

"What I think of Abe Lincoln? What I think of Mr. Roosevelt? Dere de color come up again. De black say Mr. Lincoln de best President us ever have; de white say us never have had and never will have a President equal of Mr. Roosevelt."

United States. Work Projects Administration

Project #1655
W.W. Dixon
Winnsboro, S.C.

CHARLIE ROBINSON

Ex-Slave 87 Years Old.

Charlie Robinson lives nine miles northwest of Winnsboro, S.C., on lands of Mr. R.W. Lemmon. There is one other occupant in the four-room house, John Giles, a share cropper. The house has two fireplaces, the brick chimney being constructed in the center of the two main rooms. The other two rooms are shed rooms. Charlie ekes out a living as a day laborer on the farm.

"They been tellin' me to come to de social circle and see 'bout my pension but I never is got dere. It been so hot, I hate to hotfoot it nine miles to Winnsboro and huff dat same distance back on a hot summer day.

"Glad you come out here but sorry of de day, 'cause it is a Friday and all de jay-birds go to see de devil dat day of de week. It's a bad day to begin a garment, or quilt or start de lye hopper or 'simmon beer keg or just anything important to yourself on dat day. Dere is just one good Friday in de year and de others is given over to de devil, his imps, and de jay-birds. Does I believe all dat? I believes it 'nough not to patch dese old breeches 'til tomorrow and not start my 'simmon beer, when de frost fall on them dis fall, on a Friday.

"You wants me to set down so you can ask me sumpin'? I'll do dat! Of course I will! (He proceeded to do so—wiping his nose on his sleeve and sprawling down on the doorsill). My pappy name George, black George they call him in slavery time, 'cause dere was a small yallow slave on de place, named George. My mammy name Ca'line. My pappy b'long to de McNeals and my mammy b'long to Marse Joe Beard. His wife was my mistress. Her name Miss Gracie. 'Nitials? Dat sumpin' not in my lingo, Boss. You want to know what my pappy's old marster name? Seem to me they call him Marse Gene, though it been so long I done forgot. When my marster went to de war him got a ball through his leg. Bad treatment of dat leg give him a limp for de balance of his days. White folks call him 'Hoppin' Joe Beard' and sometime 'Lopin' Joe'.

"Marster and mistress have two chillun. I play marbles wid them and make mud pies. Deir names was Marse Willie and Miss Rhoda.

"My brudders and sisters was Jeff, Roland, Jane and Fannie. All dead 'cept Fannie. Her marry a big, long nigger name Saul Griffin. Last I heard of them, they was livin' in Columbia, S.C.

"I start workin' in de field de second year of de war, 1862. It sho' made me hungry. I 'members now, how I'd git a big tin cupful of pot liquor from de greens, crumble corn bread in it at dinner time and 'joy it as de bestest part of de dinner. Us no suffer for sumpin' to eat. I go all summer in my shirt-tail and in de winter I have to do de best I can, widout any shoes. Ever since then, I just lak to go barefooted as you sees me now.

"My pappy git a pass and come to see mammy every Saturday night. My marster had just four slave houses on de place. 'Spect him have 'bout eight women, dat men come from other places to see and marry them and have chillun. I doesn't 'member nary one of de women havin' a husband livin' wid her every night.

"Who do de plowin'? Women and boys do de plowin'. Had good 'nough houses, though they was made of logs, 'cup and saddled' at both ends, and covered wid white oak board shingles. Had stick and mud chimneys.

"De Yankees made a clean sweep of everything, hosses, mules, cows, hogs, meat and 'lasses. Got so mad when they couldn't find any salt, they burn up everything. Pull Marse Joe's beard, just 'cause him name Beard. De one dat do dat was just a smart aleck and de cap'n of de crowd shame him and make him slink 'way, out de house.

"When freedom come, Marse Joe stay one year, then leave. Sell out and move to Walhalla and us move to pappy on de McNeal place. Dat year us all jined de church, Union Church. I now b'longs to New Hope Methodist Church. Us nex' move to Mr. Bill Crawford's place. Mr. Crawford got to be school commissioner on de 'publican ticket and white folks call him scalawag. Him have pappy and all de colored folks go to de 'lection box and vote. Ku Klux come dere one night and whip every nigger man they could lay deir hands on. Things quiet down then but us no more go to de 'lection box and vote.

"'Bout dis time thoughts of de gals got in my head and

feets at de same time. I was buyin' a biled shirt and celluloid collar, in Mr. Sailing Wolf's store, one Saturday, and in walked Ceily Johnson. I commence to court her right then and dere, befo' I ever git inside dat shirt and collar. Her have dark skin and was good to look at, I tell you. I de-sash-shay 'bout dat gal, lak a chicken rooster spread his wing 'round a pretty black pullet, 'til I wear out her indifference and her make me happy by marryin' me. Her was too good lookin' and too bad doin', though, for me. She left by de light of de moon when us was livin' on de Cummings place, 'bove town. Excuse me now, dat's still a fresh subject of torment to me. Let's talk 'bout chances of gittin' dat pension, when I can git another clean white shirt, lay 'round de white folks again, and git dis belly full of pot liquor."

Project #1655
W.W. Dixon.
Winnsboro, S.C.

AL ROSBORO

Ex-Slave 90 Years Old.

Al Rosboro, with his second wife, Julia, a daughter, and six small grandchildren, lives in a three-room frame house, three hundred yards east of the Southern Railway track and US #21, about two miles south of Woodward, S.C., in Fairfield County. Mr. Brice gives the plot of ground, four acres with the house, to Al, rent free. A white man, Mr. W.L. Harvey does the ploughing of the patches for him. Al has cataracts on his eyes and can do no work. Since this story was written he has received his first old age pension check of eight dollars from the Social Welfare Board in Columbia, S.C.

"Does I know what a nonagenarian is? No seh, what dat? Old folks? Well, dats a mighty long name and I been here a mighty long time. Glad you say it's a honor and a privilege by de mercy of de Lord. I's thankful! You wants to know where I was born and who my white folks then?

"I was born just one and a half mile b'low White Oak, S.C., on de old Marse Billie Brice place. My pappy b'long to old Miss Jennie Rosboro, but mammy b'long to Marse

William Brice. Her name Ann. My old mistress name Mary, daughter of de Simontons, on Dumpers Creek.

"You wants de fust thing I 'members, then travel 'long de years 'til I come to settin' right here in dis chair. Well, reckon us git through today? Take a powerful sight of dat pencil to put it all down.

"Let me see. Fust thing I 'members well, was a big crowd wid picks and shovels, a buildin' de railroad track right out de other side of de big road in front of old marster's house. De same railroad dat is dere today. When de fust engine come through, puffin' and tootin', lak to scare 'most everybody to death. People got use to it but de mules and bosses of old marster seem lak they never did. A train of cars a movin' 'long is still de grandest sight to my eyes in de world. Excite me more now than greyhound busses, or airplanes in de sky ever do.

"I nex' 'members my young misses and young marsters. Dere was Marse John; he was kilt in de war. Marse Jim, dat went to de war, come back, marry, and live right here in Winnsboro. Marse Jim got a grandson dat am in de army a sailin' air-ships. Then dere was Marse William; he moved off. One of de gals marry a Robertson, I can't 'member her name, tho' I help her to make mud pies many a day and put them on de chicken coop, in de sun, to dry. Her had two dolls; deir names was Dorcas and Priscilla. When de pies got dry, she'd take them under de big oak tree, fetch out de dolls and talk a whole lot of child mother talk 'bout de pies, to de Dorcas and Priscilla rag dolls. It was big fun for her tho' and I can hear her laugh right now lak she did when she mince 'round over them dolls and pies. Dere was some poor folks livin' close by and she'd send me over to 'vite deir chillun over to play wid her. They was name Marshall. Say they come from Virginny and was kin to de highest judge in de land. They was poor but they was proud. Mistress felt sorry for them but they wouldn't 'cept any help from her.

"Well, when I git twelve years old, marster give me to his son, Marse Calvin, and give Marse Calvin a plantation dat his son, Homer, live on now. I 'member now old marster's overseer comin' to de field; his name was McElduff. Him say: 'Al, Marse William say come to de house'. I goes dere on de run. When I git dere, him 'low: 'Calvin, I wants you to take Al, I give him to you. Al, you take good care of your young marster'. I always did and if Marse Calvin was livin' he'd tell you de same.

"I forgit to tell you one thing dat happen down dere befo' I left. Dere was a powerful rich family down dere name Cockrell; I forgits de fust name. Him brudder tho', was sheriff and live in Winnsboro. Dere was a rich Mobley family dat live jinin' him, two miles sunrise side of him. One day de Cockrell cows got out and played thunder wid Mr. Mobley's corn. Mr. Mobley kilt two of de cows. Dat made de Cockrells mad. They too proud to go to law 'bout it; they just bide deir time. One day Marse Ed Mobley's mules got out, come gallopin' 'round and stop in de Cockrell wheat field. Him take his rifle and kill two of them mules. Dat made Mr. Mobley mad but him too proud to go to law 'bout it. De Mobley's just bide deir time. 'Lection come 'round for sheriff nex' summer. No Cockrell was 'lected sheriff dat time. You ask Mr. Hugh Wylie 'bout dat nex' time him come to de Boro. Him tell you all 'bout it.

"Dat call to my mind another big man, dat live 'bove White Oak then, Marse Gregg Cameron. He was powerful rich, wid many slaves. Him lak to bar-room and drink. Him come by marster's house one day, fell off his hoss and de hoss gallop on up de road. Dat was de fust drunk man I ever see. Marster didn't know what to do; him come into de house and ask Mistress Mary. Him tell her him didn't want to scandal de chillun. She say: 'What would de good Samaritan do?' Old marster go back, fetch dat groanin', cussin', old man and put him to bed, bathe his head, make Sam, de driver, hitch up de buggy, make West go wid him, and take Marse Gregg home. I never see or hear tell of dat white man anymore, 'til one day after freedom when I come down here to Robinson's Circus. Him drop dead dat day at de parade, when de steam piano come 'long a tootin'. 'Spect de 'citement, steam, and tootin', was too much for him.

"Niggers never learn to read and write. It was 'ginst de law. White folks fear they would write deir passes and git 'way to de free states.

"Us slaves 'tend Concord Church, tho' Marse Calvin jine de Seceders and 'tend New Hope. Why us go to Concord? 'Cause it too far to walk to New Hope and not too far to walk to Concord. Us have not 'nough mules for all to ride, and then de mules need a rest. I now b'longs to Bethany Presbyterian Church at White Oak. Yes sah, I thinks everybody ought to jine de church for it's de railroad train to git to hebben on.

"Marse Calvin went to de war. Him got shot thru de hand. Yankees come and burn up everything him have. Wheeler's men just as bad.

"After freedom I got mannish. Wid not a drop of blood in me but de pure African, I sets out to find a mate of de pure breed. 'Bout de onliest place I could find one of dis hatchin', was de Gaillard quarter. I marry Gabrielle. Live fust years at de Walt Brice McCullough place, then move to de Vinson place, then to de preacher Erwin place. Dat was a fine preacher, him pastor for Concord. Him lak to swap hosses. When him come down out de pulpit him looks 'round, see a hoss him lak, soon as not him go home to dinner wid de owner of dat hoss. After dinner him say: 'If it wasn't de Sabbath, how would you trade dat hoss for my hoss?' More words pass between them, just supposin' all de time it was Monday. Then Mr. Erwin ride back dere nex' day and come back wid de hoss him took a fancy for.

"Mr. Erwin move when he git a call to Texas. I moves to de Bob Sinonton place. From dere I goes to de Jim Brice place, now owned by young Marse James Brice. I been dere 32 years. Gabrielle and me generate thirteen chillun, full blooded natural born Africans, seven boys and six gals. Then Gabrielle die and I marry Julia Jenkins. Us have five chillun, one boy and four gals. I's done a heap for my country. I wants Mr. Roosevelt to hear 'bout dat; then maybe him make de country do sumpin' for me."

Project #1655
W.W. Dixon
Winnsboro, S.C.

TOM ROSBORO

Ex-Slave 79 Years Old.

Tom Rosboro lives with his daughter, Estelle Perry, in a three-room frame house, on Cemetery Street, Winnsboro, S.C. The house stands on a half-acre plot that is used for garden truck. Estelle owns the fee in the house and lot. Tom peddles the truck, eggs, and chickens, in the town and the suburban Winnsboro mill village.

"My pappy was name Tom, just lak I is name Tom. My mammy was name Sarah but they didn't b'long to de same marster. Pappy b'long to old Marse Eugene McNaul. Mammy b'long to old Marse John Propst. De ownership of de child followed de mammy in them days. Dat throwed me to be a slave of old Marse John Propst.

"My young marsters was name Marse Johnnie, Marse Clark, Marse Floyd, and Marse Wyatt. I had two young misses. Miss Elizabeth marry a McElroy and Miss Mamie marry a Landecker. You know Marse Ernest Propst dat run dat ladies' garment store and is a member of de Winnsboro Town Council? Yes? Well, dat is one of Marse Floyd Propst chillun.

"I hear mammy say dat daddy's mistress was name Miss Emma but her mistress and my mistress was name Miss Margaret. My daddy have to have a pass every time he come to see mammy. Sometime they give him a general pass for de year. Sometime him lose de pass and then such a gwine on you never did see de lak. Make more miration (hullabaloo) over it than if they had lost one of de chillun. They was scared de patarollers (patrollers) would come ketch him, and lay de leather whip on his naked back. He wouldn't dare stay long. Him would go back soon, not on de big road but through de woods and fields, so as not to meet de patarollers.

"Who was my brothers and sisters and where is they? Brother Ben and Sister Mamie is dead and in glory. Dat's all de chillun mammy had a chance to have, 'cause she was a good woman and would never pay any 'tention to de men slaves on de Propst place. Her was faithful to pappy through thick and thin, whichever it be.

"I doesn't 'member much 'bout de Yankees, though I does 'members de Ku Klux. They visit pappy's house after freedom, shake him, and threaten dat, if him didn't quit listenin' to them low-down white trash scalawags and carpetbaggers, they would come back and whale de devil out of him, and dat de Klan would take notice of him on 'lection day.

"When I was 'bout seventeen years old, I come to de Boro (Winnsboro) one Saturday evenin' and seen a tall willowy gal, black she was but shiny, puttin' them foots of her'n down on de pavement in a pretty gamecock pullet kind of way, as if to say: 'Roosters look at me.' I goes over to Mr. Landecker's store, de Mr. Landecker dat marry Miss Mamie Propst, and I begs him to give me a cigar.

I lights dat cigar and puts out after her. I ketches up wid her just as she was comin' out of Mr. Sailing Wolfe's Jew store. I brush up 'ginst her and say: 'Excuse me lady.' Her say: 'I grants your pardon, Mister. I 'spects smoke got in your eyes and you didn't see me.' I say: 'Well, de smoke is out of my eyes now and they will never have sight for any other gal but you as long as I live.' Black as she was, her got red in de face and say: 'Who is you?' I say: 'Tom Rosboro. What might be your name, lovely gal?' Her say: 'My name is Mattie Nelson.' I say: 'Please to meet you, Sugar Plum.' Her say: 'I live down at Simpson's Turnout. Glad to have you come down to see me sometime.' After dat us kep' a meetin' in Winnsboro, every Saturday, 'til one day us went 'round to Judge Jno. J. Neils' law office and him married us. Me and Mat have our trials and tribulations and has went up and down de hills in all kind of weather. Us never ceased to bless dat day dat I run into her at Mr. Sailing Wolfe's store.

"How come I name Rosboro? I just picked it up as a mighty pretty name. Sound better than Propst or McNaul and de Rosboro white folks was big buckra in dat time.

"Us had lots of chillun; raise some and lost some. I have a son, Charlie, dat's a barber in Washington, D.C. Lucy, a daughter, marry Tank Hill. Nan marry Banks Smith. Estelle marry Jim Perry but her is a widow now. Her bought a house and lot wid de insurance money from Dr. McCants. She has a nice house on Cemetery Street, wid water and 'lectric lights. Her got four chillun. When my wife die, two years ago, I move in wid Estelle and her four chillun. Her make money by washin' and ironin' for de white folks. Me and de chillun picks cotton and 'tends to de makin' and de peddlin' of garden truck and sich lak.

Ah, us is a happy family but I ain't 'bove usin' some of dat old age pension money, if I can git it."

Project #1655
W.W. Dixon
Winnsboro, S.C.

REUBEN ROSBOROUGH

Ex-Slave—82 Years, 3 Months Old

"No sir, I can 'member nothin' 'bout de State of Verginny, where pappy said us was born. He told me, when I was 'bout two years old he and mammy Kitty was took from somewhar in dat state to Richmond, wid de understandin' to sell us as a family, and to give a man name Johnson, de preference. He say de trader couldn't find de man Johnson, and sold us to my marster, John Rosborough. My pappy name William, my brothers, Tom and Willie and my sisters, Mary and Alice.

"My marster was a kind and tender man to slaves. You see a man love hosses and animals? Well, dat's de way he love us, though maybe in bigger portion, I 'low. Marster John never marry. Set down dere dat he was good enough to buy my old gran' mammy Mary, though she never could do much work.

"Us knowed dat our gran'pappy was a white man back in Verginny, but dat was her secret, dat she kept locked in her breast and carried it wid her to de grave. You say I's very light color myself? So I is, so was she, so was pappy.

Ease your mind, us had none of de white Rosborough in us. Us come on one side from de F.F.V.'s. I's proud of dat, and you can put down dere dat deres no poor white trash blood in dese old veins, too.

"De last part of de war I worked some in de field, but not enough to hurt. My Marster was a Presbyterian, b'longed to Aimwell Church. Two or three acres in cemetery dere now, but they done move de church into de town of Ridgeway.

"Money was not worshipped then like it is now. Not much use of it. Marster raised all we eat and made all we wear right dere on de place, 'bout five miles north of Ridgeway.

"I guess Marster John had forty slaves. Us live in two-story log house wid plank floor. Marster John die, us 'scend to his brother Robert and his wife Mistress Mary. I played wid her chillun. Logan was one and Janie the other. My marster and mistress was good to me. I use to drive de mules to de cotton gin. All I had to do was to set on de long beam and crack my whip every now and then, and de mules would go 'round and 'round. Dere was three hundred and seventy-six acres in dat place. I own part of it today. I b'longs to Good Hope Church. I sure believes in de Lord, and dat His mercies is from everlastin' to everlastin' to them dat fears Him.

"'Member but little 'bout de war for freedom, 'cept dat some of de slaves of marster was sent to de front to use pick and shovel to throw up breast works, and things of dat nature. My pappy was de foreman and stayed at home, carry on whilst Marster Robert go.

"'Deed I recollects 'bout de Yankees. They come and ask my pappy, de foreman, where was de mules and hosses hid out? Pappy say he don't know, he didn't carry them off. They find out a boy dat knowed; make him tell, and they went and got de mules and hosses. They took everything and left.

"Doctor Scott was our doctor. Dere was in them days lots of rattlesnakes; had to be keerful of them. Then us hear lots and had lots of chills and fever. They found de remedy, but they was way off 'bout what make them come on you. Some 'low it was de miasma dat de devil bring 'round you from de swamp and settle 'round your face whilst you sleep, and soon as he git you to snore you sniffed it to your liver, lights and gall, then dat make bile, and then you was wid de chills a comin' every other day and de fever all de day. Marster Doctor Hayne done find out dat de skeeter bring de fever and de chills, and funny, he 'low dat it is de female skeeter bite dat does de business. You believe dat? I didn't at first, 'til old Doctor Lindor tell me dat it was no harder to believe than dat all disease come into de world when a female bite a apple in de garden of Eden.

"I think Mr. Lincoln was raised up by de Lord, just like Moses, to free a 'culiar people. I think Mr. Roosevelt is de Joshua dat come after him. No president has done as much for de poor of both races as de one now president. God bless him and 'stain him in his visions and work to bring de kingdom of heaven into and upon de earth."

United States. Work Projects Administration

Project #-1655
C.S. Murray
Charleston, S.C.

Approx. 430 Words.

WILLIAM ROSE

Going Down To Die
(Folklore) Story Told By Ex-Slave

Boss Man, you talk about de brave soldier who been in de last big war and how dey look death in de eye and spit on him. I ain't see dat war. It been 'cross de water. But I know sump'en 'bout de Civil War. I been young lad when de big gun shoot and de Yankee pile down from de north.

Talk 'bout being brave. De bravest thing I ever see was one day at Ashepoo junction. Dat was near de end of de war. Grant was standing up before Richmond; Sherman was marching tump-tump through Georgia. I was a stripling lad den and boy-like I got to see and hear everything. One day more than all, de overseer sent my pappy to Ashepoo junction to get de mail. I gone 'long wid him. Seem like I jest had to go dat day.

I member dat morning well. When I get to de junction de train start to come in. What a lot of train! De air fair smoke up wid dem. They come shouting in from Charleston, bound up-country.

I stand wid my pappy near de long trestle, and see de train rock by. One enjine in front pulling one in de back pushing, pushing, pushing. De train load down wid soldier. They thick as peas. Been so many a whole ton been riding on de car roof. They shout and holler. I make big amaze to see such a lot of soldier—all going down to die.

And they start to sing as they cross de trestle. One pick a banjo, one play de fiddle. They sing and whoop, they laugh; they holler to de people on de ground, and sing out, "Good-bye." All going down to die.

And it seem to me dat is de most wonderful sight I ever see. All them soldier, laughing light, singing and shouting dat way, and all riding fast to battle.

One soldier man say in a loud voice: "Well, boys we going to cut de Yankee throat. We on our way to meet him and he better tremble. Our gun greeze up, and our bayonet sharp. Boys we going to eat our dinner in hell today."

I turn to my pappy and ax him how can man act like dat when they going down to die. He answer me: "Dat ain't nutting. They n'use to dat. Ain't you know soldier different?"

But I say: "Pappy, you hear dem talk 'bout eat dinner in hell?"

He answer me back: "They been in de army 'long time. They don't study hell anymore."

De train still rumble by. One gang of soldier on de top been playing card. I see um hold up de card as plain as day, when de luck fall right. They going to face bullet, but yet they play card, and sing and laugh like they in their own house ... All going down to die.

De train pull 'cross de trestle. I stand up and watch um till he go out of sight 'round de bend. De last thing I hear is de soldier laugh and sing ... All going down to die.

SOURCE: Interview with William Rose, 80, ex-slave of Edisto Island, S.C., in 1936.

United States. Work Projects Administration

Project #1655
W.W. Dixon
Winnsboro, S.C.

BENJAMIN RUSSELL
Ex-Slave 88 Years.

"I was born fourteen miles north of Chester, S.C. the property of Mrs. Rebecca Nance. After eighty-eight years, I have a vivid recollection of her sympathy and the ideal relations she maintained with her slaves.

"My father was just Baker, my mother just Mary. My father was bought out of a drove of slaves from Virginia. I have been told my mother was born on the Youngblood place. (Youngblood name of my mistress' people in York County.) My father was a slave of a Mr. Russell and lived two or three miles from the Nance place, where mother lived. He could only visit her on a written pass. As he was religiously inclined, dutiful and faithful as a slave, my mother encouraged the relation that included a slave marriage between my father and mother. My mother in time, had a log house for herself and children. We had beds made by the plantation's carpenter. As a boy I remember plowing from sun to sun, with an hour's intermission for dinner, and feeding the horses.

"Money? Yes, sometimes white folks and visitors

would give me coppers, 3-cent pieces, and once or twice dimes. Used them to buy extra clothing for Sundays and fire crackers and candy, at Christmas. We had good food. In the busy seasons on the farm the mistress saw to it that the slaves were properly fed, the food cooked right and served from the big kitchen. We were given plenty of milk and sometimes butter. We were permitted to have a fowl-house for chickens, separate from the white folks. We wore warm clothes and stout brogan shoes in winter; went barefooted from April until November and wore cotton clothes in summer. The master and some of the women slaves spun the thread, wove the cloth and made the clothes. My mother lived in a two-story farm house. Her children were: William, Mattie and Thomas. We never had an overseer on the place. Sometimes she'd whip the colored children, but only when it was needed for correction.

"Yes, sir, I went with my young master, William, to Chester Court House, and saw slaves put on a block and auctioned off to the highest bidder, just like land or mules and cattle. Did we learn to read and write? We were taught to read, but it was against the law to teach a slave to write. The Legislature passed an act to that effect. A number of cases in which slaves could write, the slave would forge a pass and thereby get away to free territory. They had a time getting them back. On one occasion I run in on my young master, William, teaching my Uncle Reuben how to write. They showed their confusion.

"All slaves were compelled to attend church on Sunday. A gallery around the interior of the church, contained the blacks. They were permitted to join in the singing. Favorite preacher? Well, I guess my favorite preacher was Robert Russell. He was allowed sometimes to use the white folks school, which wasn't much in those days, just a little log house to hold forth in winter. In summer he got permission to have a brush arbor of pine tops, where large numbers came. Here they sang Negro spirituals. I remember one was called: 'Steal away to Jesus.'

"Runaway slaves? Yes, we had one woman who was contrary enough to run away: Addie, she run off in the woods. My mistress hired her out to the McDonald family. She came back and we had to pelt and drive her away.

"How did we get news? Many plantations were strict about this, but the greater the precaution the alerter became the slaves, the wider they opened their ears and the more eager they became for outside information. The sources were: Girls that waited on the tables, the ladies' maids and the drivers; they would pick up everything they heard and pass it on to the other slaves.

"Saturday afternoons? These were given to women to do the family washing, ironing, etc., and the men cut fire wood, or worked in the garden, and special truck crops. Christmas? Christmas was a holiday, but the fourth of July meant very little to the slave people. Dances? There was lots of dancing. It was the pastime of the slave race. The children played shimmy and other games, imitating the white children, sometimes with the white folks.

"The master and mistress were very particular about the slave girls. For instance, they would be driving along and pass a girl walking with a boy. When she came to the house she would be sent for and questioned something like this: 'Who was that young man? How come you with him? Don't you ever let me see you with that ape again. If you cannot pick a mate better than that I'll do the picking for you.' The explanation: The girl must breed good strong serviceable children.

"No, I never saw a ghost, but there was a general belief among the race in ghosts, spirits, haunts and conjuration. Many believe in them yet. I can never forget the fright of the time my young master, William was going off to the war. The evening before he went, a whippoorwill lighted on the window sill and uttered the plaintive 'whip-poor-will.' All the slaves on the place were frightened and awed and predicted bad luck to Master Will. He took sick in war and died, just wasted away. He was brought back in rags toward the end of the struggle.

"Mistress always gave the slaves a big dinner on New Year's Day and talked to us out of the catechism. She impressed on us after dinner that time, that we were free. Some were sorry, some hurt, but a few were silent and glad. I and many of the others had been well treated. When we were sick she visited us and summoned a doctor the first thing, but the remedies those days were castor oil, quinine, turpentine, mustard plaster and bleeding."

Project 1885 -1-
District #4
Spartanburg, S.C.
May 29, 1937

JOE RUTHERFORD
Folk-Lore: Ex-Slave

"I was born about 1846, 'cause I was in de war and was 19 years old when de war was over. I went to Charleston with my master, Ros Atwood, my mistress's brother. My mistress was Mrs. Laura Rutherford and my master at home was Dr. Thomas Rutherford. We was on Morris Island.

"My father was Allen Rutherford and my mother Barbara Rutherford. My daddy had come from Chili to this country, was a harness maker, and belonged awhile to Nichols. We had a good house or hut to live in, and my work was to drive cows till I was old 'nough to work in de fields, when I was 13. Then I plowed, hoed cotton, and hoed corn 'till last year of war and den went to Charleston.

"Master paid us no money for work. We could hunt and fish, and got lots of game around there. We had dogs but our master didn't like hounds.

"Col. Daryton Rutherford, doct's son, had me for a 'pet' on the place. They had overseers who was sometimes bossy but they wouldn't allow dem to whip me. One old nigger named 'Isom', who come from Africa, was whipped mighty bad one day. The padderollers whip me one night when I went off to git a pair of shoes for an old lady and didn't git a pass. I was 16 years old then.

"Doctor Rutherford had several farms—I reckon around 2,000 acres of land. We didn't have church nor school but sometimes we had to go to de white folks church and set in the gallery. We didn't learn to read and write. The mistress learnt some of de nigger chaps to read and write a little.

"We had Saturday afternoons off to wash up and clean up. When Christmas come the doctor would give us good things to eat. When we was sick he give us medicine, but some of de old folks would make hot teas from root herbs.

"We had old time corn-shuckings before and after freedom. We made sure enough corn den and lots of it— had four cribs full. When freedom come, the old man had fallen off a block and was hurt, so one of de overseers told us we was free and could go if we wanted to. Some of dem stayed on and some got in the big road and never stopped walking. Then we worked for $1/3$ share of the crops; had our little patch to work, too.

"I was 31 years old when I married first time. Was living in Mollohon. Her name was Leana and she belonged to Madison Brooks's family, as waiting girl. I was married twice, but had 13 children all by my first wife. I have 14 grandchildren, and so many great-grandchildren I can't count them.

"When de Ku Klux was in dat country I lived wid a

man who was one of them. The first I knew about it was when I went down to de mill, de mule throwed me and de meal, and down de road I went to running and met a Ku Klux. It was him.

"I think Abe Lincoln and Jeff Davis good men, but don't know much about dem.

"I join de church when I was 68 years old 'cause God sent me to do it. I believe all ought to join church."

> SOURCE: Joe Rutherford (92), Newberry, S.C.; Interviewer: G. Leland Summer, Newberry, S.C.

United States. Work Projects Administration

Project 1885 -1-
District #4
Spartanburg, S.C.
June 7, 1937

LILA RUTHERFORD

Folk-Lore: Ex-Slave

"I was born about 1849 in the Dutch Fork section of Newberry County, S.C. I was slave of Ivey Suber and his good wife. My daddy was Bill Suber and my mammy was Mary Suber. I was hired by Marse Suber as a nurse in the big house, and I waited on my mistress when she was sick, and was at her bed when she died. I had two sisters and a brother and when we was sold they went to Mr. Suber's sister and I stayed with him.

"My master was good to his slaves. He give them plenty to eat, good place to sleep and plenty of clothes. The young men would hunt lots, rabbits, possums, and birds. My white folks had a big garden and we had eats from it. They was good cooks, too, and lived good. We card and spin and weave our own clothes on mistress's spinning wheels.

"Marse Suber had one overseer who was good to us. We went to work at sun-up and worked 'till sun-down, none of us worked at night. We sometimes got a whipping when we wouldn't work or do wrong, but it wasn't bad.

"We never learned to read and write. We had no church and no school on the plantation, but we could go to the white folk's church and sit in the gallery. Some of us was made to go, and had to walk 10 miles. Of course, we never thought much about walking that far. I joined the church because I was converted; I think everybody ought to join the church.

"The patrollers rode 'round and ketched slaves who ran away without passes. They never bothered us. When our work was over at night, we stayed home, talked and went to sleep. On Saturday afternoons white folks sometimes give us patches of ground to work, and we could wash up then, too. We raised corn on the patches and some vegetables. On Sunday we just rested and went to neighbor's house or to church. On Christmas we had big eats.

"Corn-shuckings and cotton-pickings always had suppers when work was done. Master made whiskey up at his sister's place, and at these suppers he had whiskey to give us.

"When we was sick we had a doctor—didn't believe much in root teas.

"I married when I was 15 years old at a white man's place, Mr. Sam Cannon's. A negro man named Jake Cannon married us. Supper was give us by Mr. Sam Cannon after it was over.

"When freedom came, my mother moved away, but I stayed on.

"I think Abraham Lincoln was a good man, and Jeff

Davis was a good man. I don't know anything about Booker Washington."

SOURCE: Lila Rutherford (86), Newberry, S.C., RFD
Interviewer: G. Leland Summer, 1707 Lindsey St., Newberry, S.C.

United States. Work Projects Administration

Project #-1655
Mrs. Genevieve W. Chandler
Murrells Inlet, S.C.
Georgetown County

FOLKLORE

SABE RUTLEDGE

(Testimony given by old man born 1861, The Ark Plantation.
Horry County—owned by Mr. John Tillman)

"Fust thing I realize to remember, I nuster cry to go to the old boss—old Massa—for sugar. Massa say:

"'Martha, what Newman (he call me that) crying for?' Ma say, 'Wanter come to you for sugar!'

"'Bring the boy here, Martha!'

"He gi'e me sugar.

"Boil salt? Pump! Pump! Pump it! Had a tank. Run from hill to sea. Had a platform similar to wharf. And pump on platform. Fetch good high. Go out there on platform. Force pump. My Grandmother boil salt way after Freedom. We tote water. Tote in pidgin and keeler—make out of cedar and cypress. No 'ting to crove 'em (groove 'em) compass. Dog-wood and oak rim. Give it a lap. (This was his description, with pantomime, of the way pidgin and keelers were made by plantation carpenters)

"My Grandmother had two pots going. Boil all day and all night. Biling. Boil till he ticken (thicken) Cedar paddles stir with. Chillun eat with wooden spoons. Clay pot? Just broken piece. Indian had big camping ground on beach near the Ark. After big blow you can find big piece of pot there. I see Indian. Didn't see wild one; see tame one.

"Indigo? Old man Lashie Tillman nuster plant indigo. Seed lak a flax. Put myrtle seed in with indigo to boil. Gather and boil for the traffic. All the big folkses plant that fore the rice. Rice come in circulation, do way with indigo. Nuster (used to) farm indigo just like we work our corn. Didn't have nothing but ox. And the colored folks—they came next to the ox—Hill keep advancing out. Reckon you wouldn't blieve it, but I ken cummember (Uncle Sabe stutters a bit) when all that beach been cultivate field. Must be nature for sand hill to move. Time most got too fast now for the people to live.

"Storm? Oh my Lord! Flagg Storm? Sea naturally climb right over that hill like it wasn't nothing. Water come to King Road. Reckon it would a come further if the wind didn't shift.

"Calls this 'The Ridge.' Why? I first man settle here. Oak Ridge. (It is the highest land between the Waccamaw river and the ocean.) Just name it so.

"Member the shipwreck. Two men and lady come to the Ark. Stormy time. Massa take them to town. Old anchor there now. Come a blow you kin see it. Water rise over it high tide.

"Ma tell me bout they had the to-do. Blockade at Inlet. Had 'em out to drill (The Yankees came to shore to drill.) Old man John Tillman lose all he China-a-way! (chinaware.) Every bit of his china and paints (panes of glass) out the window. Yankee gun boat sojer (soldier) to Magnolia to drill. They tack 'em (attacked 'em) to cut 'em off. When Rebs tack 'em, small boats gone back. She had to brace 'em. Shoot dem shell to brace. (Gun boat fired to frighten Rebs who were cutting Yankees off from escape) I hear old man Frank Norris—lived right beyond Vettrill Deas—I hear him (nuster come home to the Ark and trap)—I hear him say lot of 'em bog. (Ella, Agnes and Johnnie Johnson fadder been there) Bomb shell hit the hill and bury them in the sand. Had to dig out.

"Old man John Tillman my boss. Sho treat his people good. Don't see why his folks (slaves) went to blockade (tried to escape and join Yankee gun-boats). Sho treat his colored folks good. My Grandfather, Rodrick Rutledge, driver from a boy. Time he big nuff to handle it till Freedom.

"Couldn't marry widout consent of boss." (Remark from Uncle Sabe's sister, Mom Jane, who is quite acid. All her information inherited—she Freedom child) Mom Jane: "Been to devil and come back now!"

(Comparing slavery to the lower regions)

Uncle Sabe—continuing:

"Have sick house; have chillun house." (All in this section tell great tales of the 'chillun house.' Sounds a lot like the nurse houses in Russia today. All the babies were in this day nursery in care of the older women, too old for field work.) "Corn. Meat—pig, beef, fish—plenty milk." (Some cow 'coffee cow'—that is give just enough milk for the coffee.)

"Any rice?"

Aunt Jane: (interrupting) "Pick you teet (teeth) to find the rice! Great God! Now I can buy my rice!"

Uncle Sabe: "Could plant up-land rice to Ark. (This on coast away from fresh water)

"Ash cake? Meal, salt, water. Not a grease! Not a grease! See Mudder cook it many a hundred day!"

Mom Jane: "Put it in the stove today,—nothing! Rather have it any day!"

Sabe: "Wrap it in brown paper, mostly. Cows free in woods. Alligator tail good. Snail built up just like a conch (whelk). They eat good. Worms like a conch. Bile conch. Git it out shell. Grind it sausage grinder. Little onion. Black pepper. Rather eat conch than any kind of nourishment out of salt water."

Mom Jane: "Conjur? Wouldn't turn a hucks bread for 'em." (Give a crust.)

Sabe: "What God got lot out for a man he'll get it."

"Flat boat full up (with slaves trying to escape) gone down Waccamaw. Uncle Andrew Aunt the one got he eye shoot out (by patrollers) took 'em to camp on North Island. Never see so much a button and pin in my life! Small-pox in camp. Had to leave 'em.

"Captain Ben and Captain Tom fadder—look how he die! Looker the blood! Looker the people! Looker the blood! His boat call 'The Bull River.' Up and down Pee Dee river. Meet flat! Bore hole in flat and women and chillun go down! Take men off. He COME TO THIS COUNTRY. (Came down from North before Civil War) Them darnish Yankee very percruel. (Peculiar?)

"My Great-grandmother Veenia, pirate captured and took all they money in English war. (Revolution) Dem day Ladies wear bodkin fastened to long gold chain on shoulder—needle in 'em and thimble and ting. Coming down from New York to get away from English. My great grandmother little chillun. Pirate come to her Missus. Take all they money—come cut bodkin off her shoulder. Grandmother ma gone on the boat and twiss herself in Missus' skirt. Pirate put 'em off to Wilmington. Come on down settle to Pitch Landing near Socastee. Keep on till they get to Ark.

"My Great-Grandma Veenia didn't have a teet in her head—one hundred ten years old and could eat hard a bread as any we."

    Uncle Sabe Rutledge
    Burgess, S.C.—P.O.
    Horry County
    Age 76 (Born 1861)
    Ark Plantation.

Project 1655
Genevieve W. Chandler
Georgetown County, S.C.

FOLKLORE

SABE RUTLEDGE
(Ex-Slave Story)

"They call him Rogerick Rutledge for shortness. My Grandpa REAL name Jim. First time I big enough to realect (recollect) him he have on no pants but something built kinder like overall and have a apron. Apron button up here where my overall buckle and can be let down. All been dye with indigo. Have weave shirt—dye with blue indigo boil with myrtle seed. Myrtle seed must-a-did put the color in. Old brogan shoe on he foot. Old beaver hat on he head. Top of crown wear out and I member he have paste-board cover over with cloth and sew in he hat crown. My Grandmother wear these here gingham cloth call gingham twill.

"Now the chillun! I member I was a big boy grown when I get my first pants. All boy chillun wear a shirt—— long down to knee and lower. Have belt round the middle—just like you belt to hold 'em. Chillun have not a shoe! Not a shoe for chillun on us plantation to the Old Ark. First shoe I have, Pa get a cow hide and tan it. And a man name Stalvey make my first pair of shoes. I was way near bout grown. Make the sole out the thickness of the cow hide. Short quarter. No eye—just make the hole. Last! Yes man! Yes man! Yes man! Keep 'em grease! Them shoe never wear out!

"We raise all we get to eat. Hominy, cornbread, peas, potatoes, rice. Morest we plant this here yellow corn. I cry many a day bout that yellow corn! We say, 'Pa, this here yellow corn make hominy look like he got egg cook in 'em; red corn look like hominy cook in red molasses!'

"But yellow corn stronger feed! Stronger feed! And Pa know 'em.

"Sunday come go to church in that same blue shirt! Little old pole church—(gone now)—call 'Dick Green Bay Church'. (Named for a local character.) When we go to church before freedom, Mudder and them have to have the ticket.

"Old man John Tilghman at the Ark Plantation have no overseer—have 'Driver'. Most folks on Waccamaw have overseer and 'Driver'. My Pa been the Ark 'Driver.'

"Old man Zachariah Duncan been the preacher. That the same man build the first 'Heaven Gate' church after freedom. He got drift lumber on the river and on the beach. Flat 'em—make a raft and float 'em over to the hill and the man haul 'em to 'Heaven Gate' with ox. Yes. 'Heaven Gate' built outer pick up lumber.

"Before freedom Parson Glennie—he was 'Piscopal—he would come give us a service once a month on the plantation—so mother said.

"Patches of indigo all through the woods. You know

cow eat indigo. Us have too much ox! Have to haul rail all the time keep up the old fence. Woods full up with cow. Cattle loose—free. When you want beef have to hunt for 'em like we hunts deer now. I member some ox I helped broke. Pete, Bill, Jim, David. Faby was a brown. David kinder mouse color. We always have the old ox in the lead going to haul rail. Hitch the young steer on behind. Sometimes they 'give up' and the old ox pull 'em by the neck! Break ox all the time. Fun for us boys—breaking ox. So much of rail to haul!

"(You can't tell me bout this pension? Look like to me somebody trying to smother something. Letters come. Cards come. My name on outside alright. Tell me to put my name on cards and hand 'em out to my friends. Say send twenty-five cents. Next time say 'Send thirty-five cents'. He cool off then and another man—Mr. Pope come in. Got two letter from him and he tell me be still till I hear from him again. J.E. Pope. Last blank I got from Mr. Pope he say not to look for more than thirty or thirty-two dollars a month. Say there ain't going to be no two hundred a month.)

"How come I know all these Buh Rabbit story, Mudder spin you know. Have the great oak log, iron fire dog. Have we chillun to sit by the fireplace put the light-wood under—blaze up. We four chillun have to pick seed out the cotton. Work till ten o'clock at night and rise early! Mudder and Father tell you story to keep you eye open! Pick out cotton seed be we job every night in winter time—'cept Sunday! When we grow bigger, Mudder make one card. One would spin and then Mudder go to knitting. Night time picking these cotton seed out; day time in winter getting wood!

"Fall——harvest peanut, peas, 'tater!

"I member all them Buh Rabbit story! Mudder tell 'em and we laugh and wake up! They was one bout Buh Rabbit and Buh Patridge. You know Buh Patridge the onliest one get the best of Buh Rabbit!

"Buh Rabbit bet Buh Patridge (Buh Rabbit think he so sharp you know!) He bet Buh Patridge if he fly off down the road a piece and lit Buh Rabbit can find 'em.—Buh Patridge bet him he can't! So Buh Patridge take off and fly down the road a piece and lit—like a Patridge will do—lit and turn up on he back and rake the leaves over him and kiver (cover) his body all 'cept he two foots sticking up like stick!

"Now Buh Rabbit come! He hunt and he hunt and he hunt! Couldn't find 'em and he get so hot he take off he coat and hang it on Buh Patridge foots!

"He go on hunting and after while he call out,

"'Well I can't find Buh Patridge! Can't find Buh Patridge!'

"And Buh Patridge sing out,

"'Well, Buh Rabbit, here I is! You hang you coat on my feet!'

"Buh Rabbit have to pay the bet! (I don't member what the bet was). So Buh Patridge was the onliest one I ever hear bout could get the best of Buh Rabbit!

"When Father and Mudder tell them story we chillun noddin'! Some cackle out and all jump up and go back to picking out cotton seed!

"There is another one bout Buh Bear. They goes out my head. I'll think them Buh Rabbit up fore you come back Missus!"

And Uncle Sabe, who was sitting on the 'LOOK OUT' at the Floral Beach Fishery, continued to let his eyes play all over the sea like searchlights, ready to wave the black flag and march down toward the fishery holding it aloft keeping himself in a line with the fish if fish were sighted. Since way before what he called 'the big war' he and his people have eaten mullet and rice for the three fall months. His home was visited before Uncle Sabe was located and children and grand-children, wife, sister and neighbors were found seated and standing all over the kitchen floor and piazza floor and steps——each one with a generous tin plate of rice and fresh, brown, hot 'spot'———a fish not so valuable in summer but choice in fall and winter. Two hounds and a large cat worked around among the feasters for their well chewed bones.

    SOURCE: Uncle Sabe Rutledge, The Ridge, Burgess, S.C., (Horry County)
    Born first year of the Civil War.

(He owns his house and land,——some twenty-five acres under cultivation. This is located on what appears to be a 'height of land' lying between the Waccamaw and the Atlantic. Locally it is known as 'The Sand Ridge'.)

Project 1885 -1-
District #4
Spartanburg, S.C.
May 31, 1937

Edited by:
Martha Ritter

HENRY RYAN
Folk-Lore: Ex-Slaves

"I was born in Edgefield county, S.C., about 1854. I was the son of Larkin and Cheny Ryan who was the slaves of Judge Pickens Butler who lived at Edgefield Courthouse. I has some brothers and sisters, but don't remember them all. We lived in a log house with but one room. We had good beds to sleep in, and always had plenty to eat. Old Judge Butler was a good man. I was 10 years old when he died. Before then I worked in and around the house, and freedom come I stayed with the Butler family two years, then went to Dr. Maxwell's.

"In slavery time we had extra patches of ground to work for ourselves which we sometimes worked on Saturday afternoons as we had dat time off. Judge Butler used to give us a little money, too, before freedom come, for our work. We bought clothes and things we had to have. We had a big plantation garden dat the overseers planted for all on de place to eat out of.

"We used to hunt 'possums, rabbits, squirrels, wild turkeys, doves, partridges, and set traps for partridges and set box gums for rabbits. We had good food then, plenty peas, cornbread, and wild game. When winter time come we put on wool clothes and heavy shoes.

"Old Marse Butler and his mistress was good, de best folks in de country. They lived in a big house, had a girl and a boy, and over 1000 or maybe 2,000 acres of land, on several farms. One was on Saluda River. His overseers some was no good, but master wouldn't let them treat slaves cruel, just light whipping.

"We used to have to wake up at sun-up and work till sundown. We didn't learn to read and write; but we had a prayer house on de plantation where we could go to sometimes, until freedom come, then we went on to it just the same. Old man Bennefield, a nigger preacher, talked to us there. I can 'member one of de favorite songs we sung:

> 'Show pity, O Lord, forgive,
> Let e'er repentant sinner live;
> Are not thy mercies large and free,
> May not a sinner trust in Thee.'
>
> 'My crimes are great, and can't surpass,
> _____,'

"None of Major Pickens Butler's slaves ever went away from him, but some in de neighborhood did run away, and day never heard of dem again.

"The paderrollers would catch a nigger if he didn't

have a pass. Some would pass and re-pass in the road, and maybe get catched and such scuffling would go on!

"We worked on Saturday afternoons unless boss give time off to work our own little patches or do some other work we had to do. But some would frolic then and wash up for Sunday, or set around. On Sunday we went to church and talked to neighbors. On Christmas we celebrated by having a big dinner which the master give us. We had three days holiday or sometimes a week. We had New Year's Day as a special day for working, 'cause it was a sign if we worked good dat day, we would work good all de year. The white folks had corn-shuckings and cotton pickings in slavery and after freedom, too. Den would have big supper. Some neighbors walk ten miles, like walking to church or to school. Didn't think anything of walking dat far.

"Some of de games played by children were marbles, jump-rope.

"Once an old man had his dog trained to say his prayers. The dog was fed but wouldn't be allowed to eat until he put his paws in front and bow his head on dem; de old man say to him, 'No, no, you die and go to hell if you don't say your prayers.'

"Once another fellow, a nigger, said he was going to his wife's house to see her; but he had to pass his old partner's place on de way, who was dead. When he got opposite the partner's place something, maybe a ghost, came to him and wrestled with him and wouldn't let him go on to see his wife, so he come back to his master's house and stayed.

"When the slaves got sick they had doctors, and used old herbs. 'Jerusalem Ore' was a kind of herb for children, to build them up, and there was field grass roots and herb roots which was boiled and tea drunk for fevers. And 'Primer-rhine' tea which was drunk, too. Sometimes they would hang garlic around small boys and girls necks to keep away any kind of sickness.

"We didn't have schools; started them the second year after freedom. Old General Butler give us old slaves a home each and a small patch to work.

"I married when I was 21 years old, the first time in Edgefield County, now called Saluda County. I have six children, nine grand-children, and four great-grand-children.

"I think Abe Lincoln was good man and he was Providential arrangement. I think Jeff Davis was good man, same. Booker T. Washington is good man, done lots for young niggers. I rather like it now, and not slavery time. I joined church when I was 18 to turn from evil ways and to live a better life."

> SOURCE: Henry Ryan (83), Newberry, S.C.; by G. Leland Summer, Newberry, S.C.

Project 1885-1
Folklore
Spartanburg, Dist. 4
Oct. 11, 1937

Edited by:
Elmer Turnage

HENRY RYAN

Stories From Ex-Slaves

"I live in a rented three-room house with my daughter. I am too old to do much work, but I work where I can get little jobs that I can do.

"The slaves did not expect anything after Freedom, for the South was in such a bad fix. They just got jobs where they could find them. Most of them worked as share-croppers or wage hands on the farms, and have worked like this since that time. Some few have rented farms. When any moved to town they got jobs where they could.

"I never thought much about Reconstruction. Some slaves voted at first, but when Wade Hampton was elected they didn't get to vote much.

"I think the younger generation has too much freedom and doesn't stay home enough. They want to have their own way.

"Over in old Edgefield where I was raised we had plenty to eat; plenty peas, corn bread, turnips and other things. We hunted wild game, too. I was a slave of Major Pickens Butler. He was a good man and sometimes gave us a little money for our work. Our master gave us a small patch of land to work for ourselves and plant anything we wanted.

"No, I never think anything about voting. I am satisfied just to get along."

Source: Henry Ryan (N—83), Newberry, S.C.
Interviewer: G.L. Summer, Newberry, S.C. 8/18/37.

Project 1885-1
FOLKLORE
Spartanburg Dist. 4
May 25, 1937

Edited by:
Elmer Turnage

EMOLINE SATTERWHITE
Stories From Ex-Slaves

"I am bad-sick woman, in bed and can't hardly talk and can't 'member much. I was born near Broad River in de Blair section. I belonged in slavery to de Blair family. My mudder and papa was Grace and Samuel Blair, and dey belonged to Capt. Blair. When dey was sold, I was put in de house wid a good free nigger woman to raise me and to stay 'till de war was over. Den I come to de Blair house, and helped around de house. My sisters could card, spin and weave, and I helped dem wid it. I didn't have but one dress. When it got dirty, I went down to de creek and washed it and put it against de lims to dry, but I had to put it back on before it got good dry.

"When I got old enough, I worked in de field, hoeing and picking cotton."

Source: Emoline Satterwhite (82), Newberry, S.C.
Interviewer: G.L. Summer, Newberry, S.C. May 19, 1937

United States. Work Projects Administration

Project 1885-1
FOLKLORE
Spartanburg, Dist. 4
Sept. 9, 1937

Edited by:
Elmer Turnage

ALEXANDER SCAIFE

Stories Of Ex-Slaves

"Marster Charner Scaife a-laying on his bed of death is 'bout de first thing dat stuck in my mind. I felt sorry fer everybody den. Miss Mary Rice Scaife, his wife, was mean. She died a year atter. Never felt sad nor glad den; never felt no ways out of de regular way, den.

"Overseers I recollects was, Mr. Sam Hughes, Mr. Tom Baldwin, and Mr. Whitfield Davis. Mr. Baldwin was de best to me. He had a still-house out in a field whar liquor was made. I tote it fer him. We made good corn liquor. Once a week I brung a gallon to de big house to Marster. Once I got happy off'n it, and when I got dar lots of it was gone. He had me whipped. Dat de last time I ever got happy off'n Marster's jug.

"When I was a shaver I carried water to de rooms and polished shoes fer all de white folks in de house. Sot de freshly polished shoes at de door of de bed-room. Get a nickle fer dat and dance fer joy over it. Two big gals cleaned de rooms up and I helped carry out things and take up ashes and fetch wood and build fires early every day. Marster's house had five bedrooms and a setting room. De kitchen and dining-room was in de back yard. A covered passage kept dem from getting wet when dey went to de dining-room. Marster said he had rather get cold going to eat dan to have de food get cold while it was being fetched to him. So he had de kitchen and dining-room jined, but most folks had de dining-room in de big house.

"It took a week to take de cotton boat from Chester to Columbia. Six slaves handled de flat-boat. Dere was six, as I said, de boatman, two oarsmen, two steermen and an extra man. De steermen was just behind de boatman. Dey steered wid long poles on de way up de river and paddled down de river. De two oarsmen was behind dem. Dey used to pole, too, going up, and paddling going down. Seventy-five or eighty bales was carried at a time. Dey weighed around three hundred pounds apiece. In Columbia, de wharfs was on de Congree banks. Fer de cotton, we got all kinds of supplies to carry home. De boat was loaded wid sugar and coffee coming back. On Broad River we passed by Woods Ferry, Fish Dam Ferry, Hendersons Ferry and Hendersons Island and some others, but dat is all I recollect. We unloaded at our own ferry, called Scaife Ferry.

"I split rails fer fences. On Christmas we had coffee, sugar and biscuit fer breakfast."

Source: Alexander Scaife (82), Box 104, Pacolet, S.C.
Interviewer: Caldwell Sims, Union, S.C.

Project #-1655
Phoebe Faucette
Hampton County

FOLKLORE

ELIZA SCANTLING
Ex-Slave 87 Years

"If you wants to know about de slavery times," said old Aunt Eliza, "you'se sure come to de right person; 'cause I wuz right dere." The statement was easy to believe; for old Aunt Eliza's wrinkled face and stiff, bent form bore testimony to the fact that she had been here for many a year. As she sat one cold afternoon in December before her fire of fat lightwood knots, in her one-room cabin, she quickly went back to her childhood days. Her cabin walls and floor were filled with large cracks through which the wind came blowing in.

"I gits along pretty good. My chillun lives all around here, and my granddaughter that's a-standin' at the window dere, takes care of me. Den de government helps me out. It sure is a blessing, too—to have sech a good government! And 'Miss Maggie' good to me. She brought me dis wood. Brought it in her truck herself. Had a colored man along to handle it for her. But I so stiff I sometimes kin hardly move from me waist down. And sometimes in de morning when I wake, it is all I kin do to get up an' wash me face. But I got to do it. My granddaughter bring me my meals.

"I is 87 years old. I know 'cause I wuz so high when de war broke out. An' I plowed my January to July de year 'fore peace declare. I remember dat. I wuz a good big girl; but jes' a child—not married yet. Yes'm I plowed a mule an' a wild un at dat. Sometimes me hands get so cold I jes' cry. But dey all say I 'wuz a nigger what wuz a nigger!'

"In May peace declare. De first president of de country wuz Lincoln. He took his seat in March. But I work for de white people 'fore dat. On a Friday mornin' our Massa, Mr. Richard Davant come an' told us peace declare. He come an' told us hisself. I wuz in de cornhouse a-shuckin' corn to go to de mill on Saturday. After freedom all de niggers left 'cept my Mamma. My father brought us back here to Col. Alex Lawton's place at Robertville. He used to belong to Col. Lawton. Many years atter dat Col. Lawton moved to Savannah; but when he died dey brought him back here an' buried him at Robertville.

"My young Missus was de daughter of Mr. Sam Maner, my old Massa; so when she marry Mr. Davant I went wid her. Dey had bought a place in Screven, Georgia. Seven year 'fore peace declare we went to Georgia. On a Monday mornin' a colored man come along an' tell Miss Anna de Yankees had took Waynesboro. We all went to see it. De fire had left de place clean. Could pick up a pin behind it. Other than dat I see nothin'. I never see no house burn down. I never hear no gun fire. I jes' see de uniform, an' see 'em kill de hog an' sling 'em 'cross de saddle. Den when we come back to Robertville, we see de destruction left behind.

"After I git of size I mind de birds off de corn an' rice an' sech like. Den I'd take care of de turkeys. An' we'd sweep de yards. Carry de leaves off to de stable in a wheelbarrow.

"Both my missus wuz good to me. De last missus I own treat me jes' de same as her own child. I stayed right dere in de house wid her, an' if I wuz sick or anything she'd take care of me same as her own chillun. I nurse one of her chillun. An' dat child would rather be wid me than wid her own mother!"

Source: Elisa Scantling, Scotia, S.C. age 87 years.

United States. Work Projects Administration

Code No. 390166
Project No. 1885-(1)
Prepared by Mrs. Lucile Young & H. Grady Davis
Place, Florence, S.C.
Date, May 25, 1937
Typed by M.C., N.Y.A.

No Words_____
Reduced from _____ Words
Rewritten by

MARY SCOTT

Ex-Slave, About 90 years old

"Where and when were you born?"

"On Gaston Gamble place, between here and Greeleville. In da Gamble's Bible is my age. Don't know my age. Pretty much know how old, I bout 90. I wuz little girl when freedom come."

"Give the names of your father and mother."

"Father, John Davis. Mother, Tina Davis. Belonged to last mausa. Darby Fulton. Gamble sold mama and three children to Fulton. Belonged to Davis after freedom. Father belonged to Davis. Take first mausa's name. Sold to Arnold Mouzon. Didn't take Mouzon name."

"Where did your father and mother come from?"

"Right where Grandma go, Gamble place."

"Did you have any brothers and sisters?"

"James and Benjamin. All ded."

"Describe the beds and where you slept."

"Had plenty slaves. I don't know exactly how many. In dem times you know, we had to get ticket to go to see dere family."

"What kind of house did you have to live in?"

"Better dan dis. Better dan dis. Good house. Sleep on wooden bed. Straw and feather mattress."

"Do you remember anything about your grandparents or any stories told you about them?"

"I ain't know my grandmother, grandfather either."

"What work did you do in slavery times."

"Didn't do no kind of work. Mother milked, tended to de butter."

"Did you ever earn any money?"

"No money."

"What did you eat and how was it cooked?"

"Boil meat and put peas or greens, rice cooked dry, take up in plate and eat. One girl get done and wash dishes and put dem up."

"Did you ever eat any possums?"

"Yes, my brother catch possum and raccoon."

"Fish?"

"Fishing in de branch."

"Did the slaves have their own gardens?"

"Yes, sir, plant big garden, no use plant, go to dere garden and get it."

"What clothes did you wear in cold weather?"

"Thick. I could weave it with stripes and put one check one way and nother strip nother way."

"Hot weather?"

"In winter warm clothes and shoes. Had Sunday clothes. I had a green worsted dress."

"Did the slaves have a church on your plantation?"

"Go to white people church and sit out of doors and wait till dey come out and den we go in and have preaching."

"White or colored preacher?"

"White preacher."

"Was your master a good man?"

"Mr. Gamble like to drink liquor but still good people. All who I talking about good people."

"What was Mr. Gamble's name?"

"Mr. Gamble name Gatron Gamble. Son living in dat big house and grandson living down dere."

"How many children did Mr. Davis have?"

"He had some not many. Mr. Gamble had some too."

"What kind of house did Mr. Gamble live in?"

"Medium size house. All had just common house, two-story."

"What about the overseer?"

"Overseer he see dat you work soon. Driver go in de field and stay 'til 12 o'clock."

"How many acres in the plantation?"

"Don't know how many acres."

"What time did the overseer wake the slaves up?"

"Wake dem up soon. Blow horn."

"Did you have to work hard?"

"Work 'til sundown."

"Did you see any slaves punished?"

"Some punished, but I ain't never see none whip. I heard stick strike de ground and tie hands and feet. Paddle on dis side and den paddle on de other side 'til sore."

"Did you ever see any slaves sold or auctioned off?"

"My mother and us sold. Mrs. Gamble died left my mama for a daily gift. She wouldn't allow dem to whip me. I ain't know when we be sell, I wuz a baby."

"Did you see slaves in chains?"

"No chains."

"Did the slaves have a church on your plantation?"

"Yes, de Gambles make us to go to Sunday school and learn us the Sunday school lessons. I could plow. We went to white church and set down till white people go out and de old man dat tend to de church and open up de church and say come in, can't stay outside."

"Who preached for you all?"

"My uncle, Jefferie Pendergrass, mother's brother. If colored people want preacher preach, he go in dere and made de children be quiet and preach a nice sermon and have watch night but not in de church."

"Do you know any spirituals?"

"I forgets dem things. I use to be good singer but I ain't got no teeth. I ain't been looking fer dis. If you hadn't come, I'd been gone."

"Where would you have gone?"

"Just to walk about. All gone to de field and de children so bad."

"Tell about baptizing."

"Baptized by de white people."

"Did the slaves run away to the North?"

"I ain't know 'bout dat."

"What about patrollers?"

"No patarollers. Have to get ticket, whip dem if dey didn't get it. Colored people do more than white people allow. Caused dem to whip dem. My sister, my sister-in-law and girl went and tell dem dey gwine have play in white kitchen. Mr. Sam Fulton boss wouldn't go to war. My sister, sister-in-law run up in de loft and tell dem come down and dey come down and jump off de window and land in de mud hole wid dere best dress on. Mr. Fulton let dem have it in de quarters."

"Did you hear of any trouble between the master and the slaves?"

"My grandmother went off and wouldn't come back. She write that she get everyday what she could get fer Sunday."

"Did you work on Saturday evenings?"

"Some of de white people made dem work on Saturday evening. I had a uncle when white people come by going to church he hoeing his rice. Dey didn't want him work on Sunday. Miss Elizabeth Gamble tell dem he gwine to chop his rice on Sunday."

"What did you do on Sunday?"

"Go to church."

"Christmas day?"

"I don't remember what dey give on Christmas day. My family got clothes."

"What did you do at a wedding or funeral among the slaves?"

"Just say got a wife, ain't married. If anybody ded everything stop."

"What games did you play as a child?"

"I don't know what all I played."

"Do you know any funny stories?"

"No, sir, I used to tell my grands things."

"Did you ever see any ghosts?"

"I ain't believe in it, but I see dem. Jest pass by and dey want bother you. Don't know where dey come from. Dey look like people."

"You don't believe in them?"

"No, sir, but I know one thing, dey say fox gwine mad. Say cat gwine mad but dat ain't so. I ain't scared of nothing."

"You are not scared at night?"

"When de moon shining. Moon ain't shine might fall and cripple. When we holler voice way back dere."

"When the slaves became sick, who tended to them?"

"White people tended to dem. Use medicine."

"Do you make medicine out of herbs?"

"No, sir, don't make it."

"Did you ever see anybody wear a ten-cent piece around the ankle?"

"I see dem wear it, but I ain't know what fer."

"What do you remember about the war that brought you freedom?"

"I know just as good when peace declared. Gun rolled

in dat direction. Must be guns. Cook say roll thunder roll and I say de sun shine it ain't gwine rain. I wuz too little to know but my sister say every man and every woman got to work for demselves."

"What did your master say?"

"I ain't know what master say, he single man and didn't talk much."

"Did you stay with him the year after freedom?"

"No, he didn't treat my mother right."

"Any schools for Negroes?"

"Pretty good time before schools."

"Did the slaves buy any land?"

"No land bought."

"Do you remember your wedding?"

"I member jest as good 'bout my wedding. I married on Thursday night. Some white people from Kingstree and different ones come and pile it up and when I get all dem presents some one stick fire and burn it all down."

"Whom did you marry?"

"John Scott."

"Do you have any children?"

"One gone in de field and dis one."

"What are they doing?"

"Working on farms. Jane got killed in de wreck."

"Who is Jane?"

"My daughter. She wuz coming to see me. Train wreck and kill her coming from Norfolk."

"How long ago was that?"

"'Bout two years ago."

"What do you think of Abraham Lincoln?"

"I see picture of dem. Picture in dere of Lincoln."

"Now that slavery time is ended, what do you think of it?"

"I believe colored people do better in de slavery than now."

"Do you belong to the church?"

"Yes, Promise Land Baptist church."

"Why do you think people ought to go to church?"

"To have some protection and when you go in a church dat is a place for you to be taken care of. Dey ain't got no religion."

"Was the overseer 'poor white trash?'"

"I could hear de people talk 'bout him. Some like him and some don't. If I got a wife over yonder, I got to get ticket before I could go to see her. Had to work hard too."

"Let us see the picture of Lincoln."

"Dis is it." (Granddaughter shows us Aunt Mary's picture)

"Is that the one?"

"Yea, I think so."

"Let me see, dat ain't de one. Here is." (Aunt Mary showed us a picture which looked to be taken from some New York newspaper. It was probably a screen star).

"Who told you that was Lincoln?"

"Some preacher or somebody come here and tell me."

Project 1885-1
FOLKLORE
Spartanburg—Dist. 4
May 18, 1937

Edited by:
Elmer Turnage

NINA SCOTT

Stories From Ex-Slaves

"Aunt" Nina Scot sat on her front porch. She was drinking some liquid from a bottle which she said would help her trouble. Being short of breath, she was not able to talk very much. She said that she was very small at the time she was set free. "My Marster and his folks did not treat me like a nigger," she said, "they treated me like they did other white folks." She said that she and her mother had belonged to Dr. Shipp, who taught at Wofford College, that they had come here from Chapel Hill, N.C. and that she was a tarheel negro. She said that white people in slavery days had two nurses, one for the small children and one for the older ones. "Yes sir, those were certainly fine people that lived on the Campus during those days. (Wofford Col. Campus) When the 'raid' came on, people were hiding things all about their places." She referred to the Yankee soldiers who came to Spartanburg after the close of the Civil War. "My mother hid the turkeys and told me where she had hidden them." Dr. Shipp came up to Nina one day and asked her where the turkeys were hidden. She told him they were hidden behind a clump of small trees, and pointed them out to him. "Well," he said, "tell your mother to go and hide them somewhere else and not to tell you about it. You would tell the Yankees just where those turkeys were hidden." Aunt Nina recalls that Mr. and Mrs. Dr. Duncan (formerly of Wofford College) had a habit of getting a slice of bread and butter for all the neighboring children (black or white) whenever their nurses brought them to their home.

    SOURCE: "Aunt" Nina Scott, 260 N. Converse St., Spartanburg, S.C.
    Interviewer: F.S. DuPre, Spartanburg Office, Dist. 4 (May 17, 1937)

Project 1885-1
FOLKLORE
Spartanburg Dist. 4
May 25, 1937

Edited by:
Elmer Turnage

MORGAN SCURRY
Stories Of Ex-Slaves

"I was born in Newberry County, near the Laurens County line, above Chappells Depot. My father and mother were Tom and Francis Scurry and belonged as slaves to the Drury Scurry family. Dr. Drury Scurry bought them from Col. Cooper of Laurens County. He was a fine man and mighty good to his slaves. I worked around the house as a boy, and in the fields when I got old enough. Some of the nigger boys hunted 'possums, rabbits and squirrels. Dr. Scurry had 100 acres in woods. They were just full of squirrels and we killed more squirrels than you can count.

"The slaves didn't have a garden, but after the war, we stayed on wid Marse Scurry. When freedom come, he come to us in the yard where we had congregated and told us we was free and could go anywhere we wanted, but if any wanted to stay on wid him, he would pay wages. All of us stayed on wid him. He give us a one-acre patch of ground to raise anything we wanted to raise. He had white overseers during slavery, but none ever whipped us 'cause the master wouldn't let them. He had a plantation of about 300 acres and 40 or 50 slaves. They got up at sun-up and worked 'till sun-down each day, but had Saturday afternoons off when dey could do anything dey wanted to.

"There wasn't much time for learning to read and write. The white folks sometimes had niggers to go to their church and set in the back of gallery. In our neighborhood, niggers had their own church dat they made of poles and brush, and called it, 'Brush Harbor'. They made seats from small logs sawed off of rough plank.

"On Christmas day, the master would have a big dinner for his slaves and spread it out in the yard. Corn shuckings were popular and so were cotton pickings, where big eats were prepared for those who helped. They had big feasts at marriages, and even the slaves had feasts at their marriages, the master and his family taking part in the ceremonies. I was married in 1887, and at that time I was living with Mr. Renwick, and my girl with Dr. Tom Brown. Dr. Brown had us to marry in his yard in the grove, and over 200 persons was there to see it. The next day, he give us a big 'infair' with all kinds of good things to eat, presents and dances. We never had any children. After we moved to town, my wife was a nurse or midwife among some of the white families for a long time.

"In Ku Klux times, I met five or ten of them in the road one night. They never bothered me. They had long white sheets over them and the horses. Slits were cut for the head, eyes, nose and mouth.

"The niggers had an old field song: 'Give me dat good

ole time religion' which they sang most of the time. There was another song they sang: 'Dark midnight is my cry—Give me Jesus, You may have all this world, but give me Jesus.'

"Some old-time cures for the sick was—barks of cherry tree, dogwood, and olive bush, made into tea and drunk.

"I thought Abe Lincoln was a fine man, done mighty good and saved the country. Jeff Davis was a good man. Booker Washington was a great man. I think slavery was bad; yet our white folks was good to us, but some white masters was mean. I think everybody should belong to the church and be a Christian."

>SOURCE: Morgan Scurry (78), Newberry, S.C.; interviewed by:
>G.L. Summer. Newberry, S.C. May 19, 1937.

S-260-264-N
Project #935
Hattie Mobley
Richland County
South Carolina

RANSOM SIMMONS

Richland County, South Carolina.

Uncle Ransom is one of the few remaining slaves who still lives and whose mind is still clear and active. He has just passed his one-hundred and fourth birthday, was born in Mississippi, and brought to South Carolina by his master Wade Hampton, the father of the illustrious General Wade Hampton, before the Civil War.

When the war broke out and General Wade Hampton went to war Uncle Ransom cried to be allowed to follow his young master. He went and served as a body guard. Uncle Ransom learned to read the Bible while attending a night school held for slaves before freedom, and it was only in recent years that he was taught to write his name.

This old man lives alone in a shack at Taylor, a little village on the outskirts of Columbia. He is furnished with all the milk and ice cream he can eat by the Columbia Dairy. He purchases a little food with the state pension of twenty-five dollars a year paid to Negroes who served the Confederacy in some military capacity.

Uncle Ransom says his master was the kindest man in the world, and that as far as he is concerned, he has never had a worry in his life, and as he said this, his face radiated with a broad and satisfied smile.

Reference:

Personal interview with Ransom Simmons age 104.

Project #1655
Stiles M. Scruggs
Columbia, S.C.

ALFRED SLIGH

Ex-Slave 100 Years Old.

Alfred Sligh, who lives in a rented house at 1317 Gregg Street, says he was born in Newberry County, South Carolina, in 1837. His hair is white and he is feeble. He goes about the city, on fair days, collecting small sums of money from his white friends and sometimes from his own race. In this way he earns most of his income.

"My folks was slaves of the Sligh family for many years, befo' I was born. My mammy and daddy and me b'long to Butler Sligh, at de time I begin to do chores and take notice of things. I be nearly half grown when my young master, Butler Sligh, am just four years old. He die, four or five years ago. I guess you 'member, 'cause he was a powerful well-known white man. He was seventy-five years old when he die.

"De young master, he name for my old master. De old master and 'most all de white men of de neighborhood, 'round 'bout us, march off to de war in 1861. One day I see them ridin' down de big road on many hosses and they wavin' deir hats and singin': 'We gwine to hang Abe

Lincoln on a sour apple tree!' and they in fine spirits. My young master, Butler, who they call Junior at de time, he am too young to go with them so we stay home and farm. I go with him to de fields and he tell de slaves what to do. Durin' de war I see much of de soldiers who say they not quit fightin' 'til all de damn-Yankees am dead. Dis was so, durin' de first two years. After dat I see more and more of de damn-Yankees, as they pass through 'flictin' punishment on 'most everybody.

"Sho' we hear dat all Negroes am free in 1863, but dat rumor not affect us. We work on, 'til Sherman come and burn and slash his way through de state in de spring of 1865. I just reckon I 'member dat freedom to de end of my life.

"We gang up at my grandmother's cabin and she tell us it am so. We look scared, lak mules in de midst of a hornet nest, as we stood dere. We didn't wait long, for old Mistress Sligh she come 'long and say: 'Sho' it am so, you am free.' Many of de slaves, 'cludin' me, tell her we love to stay on and work as usual 'til de big white folks come. She smile and say: 'All right, maybe we be able to feed and clothe you, and when your old master git back from Virginia, maybe he will hire you!'

"When I first marry, which was at de start of de war, I marry Sarah, a slave gal on de Sligh plantation. We has several chillun, befo' she die, which was soon after we move to Columbia. De chillun, at least two boys and two gals, all git grown, but they go North a long time ago, and I never hears from them.

"When I come to Columbia in 1866, I find work on houses, and building was plentiful then. I git 'long pretty well, then, 'cause if I did not land a job, I could go to de Freedman's Aid Office at Assembly and Gervais streets and git rations and a little cash for my family. After de Freedman's Aid left town I had no trouble findin' work. And soon I was pretty prosperous. I kept that way, so long as I was able to do my share of de work.

"It was in 1913, as I was walkin' 'long Hampton Street, dat I see my present wife, Sadie. She pass by me, and smile and look and I smile and look, and she slow up a little and say: 'What's happen, big boy?' I am so tickled, I say: 'I just have to tell you:

> 'De rose am red,
> De violet's blue,
> No knife can cut
> My love in two.'

"She say; 'Pretty good, big boy, pretty good! Come 'round and see me sometime.' I answer: 'I sho' will, Peaches and Cream'. And dat am just what I did. We got married dat same year, and we have been happy, 'til I git too old and feeble to work much. She work now to de best of her ability and we somtimes has a big squeeze to pay de rent. Dat is why I'm hopin' to get de old age pension, made possible by de greatest President of them all.

"Does I recall de 'sassination of de first President dat died dat way? Yes sir, I sho' do. De first one was Abraham Lincoln, a little after de close of de war. He was shot while sittin' in a seat in de theater at Washington. James A. Garfield, was de nex' one. He was shot in de depot, at Washington. De nex' one was McKinley. He was shot while at a show place, in Buffalo."

United States. Work Projects Administration

Project #1655
W.W. Dixon,
Winnsboro, S.C.

DAN SMITH

Ex-Slave 75 Years.

Dan Smith lives in one room, rent free, of a three-room frame house, the property of his son-in-law, Jim Cason. It is situated on the southeast corner of Garden and Palmer streets in the town of Winnsboro, S.C. He is tall, thin and toothless, with watery eyes and a pained expression of weariness on his face. He is slow and deliberate in movements. He still works, and has just finished a day's work mixing mortar in the construction of a brick store building for Mr. Lauderdale. His boss says: 'The spirit is willing but the flesh is weak.' There is nothing organically wrong with Dan but he appears, in human anatomy, as Doctor Holmes's One Horse Shay must have looked the day before its final collapse.

"You been here once befo' and now here you is again. You say you wanna git additions? Well, I's told you dat I was born in Richland County, a slave of Marse John Lever and on his plantation, January de 11th day, 1862, when de war was gwine on. How I know? 'Cause my mammy and pappy told me so. They call my pappy Bob and my mammy Mary. Strange as it seem, my mistress name Mary, just de same as my mammy, tho' marster wasn't name

Bob, lak pappy. Him name Marster John and de young marster, an only child, was name Marse Jim. You better stop right dere 'til I tell you pappy no b'long to de Levers. Him b'long to de Smiths. Him name Bob Smith, after freedom. Dat's how come I be dis day, Dan Smith. You ketch de p'int? Well dats de way it was.

"Befo' pappy take a shine to mammy in slavery time, her got mixed up wid one of old Marse Burrell Cook's niggers and had a boy baby. He was as black as long-leaf pine tar. Her name him George Washington Cook but all him git called by, was Wash Cook. My full brudders was Jim, Wesley, and Joe. All of them dead and gone long ago.

"Us chillun slept on de floor. Mammy had some kind of 'traption or other, 'ginst de wall of de log house us live in, for her and de baby child to git in at night. Us have plenty to eat, sich as: peas, 'tatoes, corn bread, 'lasses, buttermilk, turnips, collards and fat meat.

"De only thing I 'member 'bout my mistress is: One day her come down to de house and see my brudder Joe sucking his thumb. Mammy tell her, her can't make him quit it. Mistress go back to de big house and come runnin' back with quinine. Her rub Joe's thumbs wid dat quinine and tell mammy to do dat once or twice a day. You ought to see dat baby's face de first time and heard him squall! It sho' stopped him sucking his thumbs!

"Clothes? Didn't need no clothes in de summer time but a shirt. In de winter, us just stood 'bout de fire. I'm talkin' 'bout us chillun, don't 'member 'bout old folks.

"Master and Mistress lived in a big white house, two stories high, tall brick chimneys at de gable ends, and wide front and back piazzas de full length of de dwelling. Us chillun had no shoes. Mammy had two pair all de time but they had wooden bottoms. Dere was no white overseers 'round, but patarollers (patrollers) ketched my pappy once, in de house, jerk him out and whup him, while mammy and us chillun yell and cry and beg them to stop.

"When de Yankees come, mammy hide us chillun under her bed 'traption. They act mighty nice to her, so she say.

"What kinda work mammy do? Her was one of de weavers. Heard her tell 'bout how they make de thread and de cloth. They had spinnin' wheels. Person turn de wheel wid de hand and walk back'ards and for'ards, drawing out de thread. Dis kind of thread, her say, was rough. Later they got a thing de spinners operate wid deir foots, settin' by de wheel and workin' it wid deir foots, sorta lak a sewing machine is run. Her 'low de thread dat come to her in de weave-room from dis kind of spinnin' was smoother and more finer than de other kind. After de yarn was spin, it was reeled off de spools into hanks and then took to de warper. Then she woofed it, warped it, and loomed it into cloth. Her make four yards in a day.

"After freedom, pappy come and take mammy and all us chillun to a farm on Cedar Creek, in dis county, Fairfield. I works dere 'til 1872, I thinks. I gits concerned 'bout dis time wid two things, jinin' wid de Lord, and jinin' wid de woman. De fust was easy. All I had to do was go to de Methodis' revival, shout a little, and jine up befo' de preacher. I just had to be convicted and convinced, but mind you, I was de one to be convinced, de other was not so easy. De Lord was easy to find and quick to take me, but de gal was hard to find and was slow to take me, 'cause she was de one to be convinced dis time, you see.

"I looks all 'round Cedar Creek. De ones I could git, I wouldn't have, and de ones I would have I couldn't git. So dere it was. I mounts old Betsy, dat was pappy's mule, one Sunday and come to Winnsboro. I spied a gal at church, 'bout de color of a ripe pumpkin after de big frosts done fall on it, hair black as a crow and meshed up and crinkled as a cucker burr. Just lookin' at her made my mouth water. Me and old Betsy raise de dust and keep de road hot from Cedar Creek to Winnsboro dat summer and fall, and when us sell de last bale of cotton, I buys me a suit of clothes, a new hat, a pair of boots, a new shirt, bottle Hoyt's cologne and rigs myself out and goes 'round and ask her to marry me. Her name Ida Benjamin. Did her fall for me right away? Did her take me on fust profession and confession lak de Lord did? No sir-ree bob! Her say: 'I got to go to school some more, I's too young. Got to see papa and mama 'bout it. Wait 'til you come nex' time and I'll tell you.' I was confused then, I gits up, gives her de cologne bottle, and mounts old Betsy, spurs her in de side, gallops, and cusses all de way back to Cedar Creek. I confess to mammy. Her laugh and say: 'Dan, you knows nothin' 'bout women and gals. Why it's mighty plain she gonna say yes, nex' time.' Just lak her say, Ida did, and us got married de end of de nex' school term, in May.

"Us had ten chillun. Dan, name for me, is at Concord, N.C. Oscar is in Concord, N.C. Lucinda marry a Haltiwanger and is comfortable in Baltimore, Md. Aurelia marry a Williams and is in Baltimore. Henrietta marry a Sawney and is in Charlotte, N.C. Lilly marry Jim Cason and live right in Winnsboro, in de house I have a room in.

"I got lots of gran'childs, too many to mention, They take after dere grandma, lak to go to school and read de Bible and go to church and Sunday School.

"Whut I have on my mind now is a pension. When a man git seventy-five years old, (I hear folks talk 'round me) dat man should not be 'lowed to work on de Supreme Court, him should be give a pension of $15,000.00 and made to stop work. Him may have chillun dat can support him, all de same, dat jedge gits his pension. Then in de name of goodness, why don't they make me quit mixing mortar when I is seventy-five years old and give me $240.00 a year? Sauce for de fat goose Supreme Court Jedge, oughta be sauce for de mortar mixer poor gander, I 'low. It look lak jestice for de rich jedge and mix more mortar for poor Dan."

Code No.
Project, 1885-(1)
Prepared by Annie Ruth Davis
Place, Marion, S.C.
Date, July 22, 1937

No. Words_____
Reduced from_____words
Rewritten by

HECTOR SMITH

Ex-Slave, 79 Years

"I born down here in Wahee Neck. Easter Avant, dat was my mammy en my father name Hector Smith. Coase I ain' never see him cause he die fore I was born, but dat what dey tell me. Dat was a pretty rough time wid de people den. I don' recollect so much bout de times back dere cause in dat day en time chillun didn' have de heap of knowledge dey have dis day en time, but I remembers seein de Yankees en de people gwine to de war. Oh, dat was a tough time cause dey use de whip in dem days. Oh, yes'um, my Massa whip my gran'mammy wid a leather strap. You see she had a knack of gwine off for some cause or another en meetin de boat what run up en down dat big Pee Dee river en bring fertilizer en all kind of goods to de peoples. Massa Randall had told her not to go nowhe' bout dat boat, but some people is sorta high strung like en dey go off anyhow no matter bout de whip. Oh, yes'um, he sho whip her like he didn' have no soul to save."

"I couldn' tell you nothin bout how many slaves Massa Randall Davis had, but I know dat he had a right smart of them. I know it cause he had so many field hands dey didn' none of em never have to work every day in de field. Oh, dey just knock bout our Massa house en see after de stock en such things as dat what time dey didn' have to work in de field."

"You knows when a thing happen so long back dere, it does vanish from a person's remembrance some of de time en den it'll wander back to you when you ain' thinkin bout it. I does recollect dat dere wasn' nothin much more for de colored peoples in dat day en time den what dey got to eat en de clothes dey had to wear. My Massa give everyone of he colored family a peck of meal en a quart of syrup en so much of meat every week en 'low em all to have a garden of dey own. Oh, dey work dey garden by de moonshine en fore light good in de mornin cause dey had to turn dey hand to dey Massa work when daylight come here. I tellin you corn bread was sweet to me in dat day en time as pound cake ever been. Wasn' never noways pickin' en choosin bout nothin. Oh, I forget bout all dem possums en rabbits dat eat right smart in dem days. Use to catch em when dey had swells of de water en dey come out de woods to hunt dry land. It just like dis, dey couldn' conceal demselves in de open fields en dat how-come we catch em so easy. Run em down wid de dogs en make em take to de water. Dat how we catch em. Dat sho was sweet eatin in dem days."

"Den we had a log house to stay in what never had but just one room en de furniture we had was worser den de house. Us beds was made wid four stumps for de corners dat had boards lay cross em to put de mattress on. Some of de colored peoples had bag mattress stuff wid hay en de others had homespun mattress what was stuff wid dis here gray moss you see in de woods. En I remembers all bout when de peoples had to cook in de fireplace cause dere wasn' much stoves in circulation in dat day en time."

"Well, I don' know so much bout dem things peoples call ghost, but I know dat I has seen things. I knows once long time back I was gwine long de road late on a evenin drivin me ox what I had hitch up to de cart en a ghost or somethin or another cause dat cart wheel to go right in de ditch. Well, de ox, he pull en he pull, but wid all me help, he couldn' never pull dat cart out. I ax some of dem people bout dere what dey reckon dat was en dey say all dey know to compare it to was a hant or a ghost. No 'mam, didn' see it, just hear it cause it come right to my back en knocked. It had been rainin en soon as it quit, de moon shine out bright as ever was day en dat when de hant turn de cart loose."

"De next thing I see was one time when me en another fellow was sleepin in de swamp. I couldn' tell whe' de moon rise den en when I come to my senses, dere was one of dem things just a danglin in de air like dese things show people have. Some people say dat was a ghost."

"Oh, de peoples didn' never worry bout no doctor den. Dey doctor was in de field in dat day en time. I gwine tell you just like I know it, all de older peoples use to get de herbs out de old fields for dey remedies. My Massa en my Missus was de ones what doctor mostly in dem times. Use to get old field ringdom, what smell like dis here mint, en boil dat en let it steep. Dat what was good to sweat a fever en cold out you. Den dere was life everlastin tea dat was good for a bad cold en cherry bark what would make de blood so bitter no fever never couldn' stand it. Dem what had de rheumatism had to take dat lion's tongue or what some peoples calls wintergreen tea en some of de time, dey take pine top en mix wid de herbs to make a complete cure. Oh, dey make it bad as dey could so as to weaken de case. Another thing dat been good for de rheumatism was dat red oak bark dat dey use to bathe de limbs wid. Willow tea was somethin good for chill en fever en catnip en sage tea was de thing for babies."

"It like I tell you de colored peoples never get no learnin but what little dey catch from de plantation men in dem night schools. Oh, dey give everyone of us a slate en slate pencil en we study dere in de quarter in de night time by de light of de fire. Studied dem Blue Back Websters. Dat was de text we know bout den."

"I tell you de truth I live so much in darkness den dat I think dat time was bout good as dis time. Didn' know no better sense den. I tell you just like I been know it, de peoples was coward like in dem days. Couldn' never pluck up no ambition to do a heap of things de people do dis day en time. Dat how-come I rather live in dis go round."

Source: Hector Smith, ex-slave, age 79, Wahee section of
Marion Co., S.C.
Personal interview, July 1937.

Code No. 390144
Project, 1885-(1)
Prepared by Annie Ruth Davis
Place, Marion, S.C.
Date, July 14, 1937

No. Words_____
Reduced from_____words
Rewritten by

HECTOR SMITH

Ex-Slave, 79 years

"I studied en studied what songs would suit, but dem old familiar hymns bout all I know dese days. You see dem old familiar hymns what de spirit sings. It just like I tell you, I put all dem other kind of songs away when I is change to a better way of livin. I does remember first one en den de other of dem frolicksome song dat my grandparents learnt me."

United States. Work Projects Administration

NOBODY BUSINESS BUT MINE

I. Rabbit in de hollow,
I ain' got no dog,
How can I catch em?
I do know! I do know!
O Me! O Mine!
Sorry dat if I leave my home,
I gwine to my shack
Wid de chicken on my back,
Nobody business but mine.

II. Rabbit in de hollow,
Ain' got no dog,
How can he catch em?
I do know! I do know!
O Me! O Mine!
Let every nigger have his way,
Gwine to his shack
Wid he chicken on his back,
Nobody business but his.

Source: Hector Smith, ex-slave, 79 years.,
Wahee section of Marion Co., S.C.
Personal interview, July 1937.

Code No.
Project, 1885-(1)
Prepared by Annie Ruth Davis
Place, Marion, S.C.
Date, July 14, 1937

No. Words_____7_____
Reduced from_____words
Rewritten by

HECTOR SMITH

Way Down In De Lonesome Valley

I. De mockin birds a singin so sweetly,
So sweetly, so sweetly.
De mockin birds a singin so sweetly,
So sweetly, so sweetly.
Way down in de lonesome valley.

II. Dey tell you one thing en dey mean another,
Mean another, mean another.
Dey tell you one thing en dey mean another,
Mean another, mean another.
Way down in de lonesome valley.

III. Some say, what make de young girls so deceivin?
So deceivin, so deceivin?

> Some say, what make de young girls so deceivin?
> So deceivin, so deceivin?
> Way down in de lonesome valley.

"Dat go way back dere. De peoples didn' have nothin more den a mouth organ to make music wid in dem times."

> Source: Hector Smith, age 79, ex-slave., Wahee section of Marion Co., S.C.
> Personal interview, July 1937.

Code No.
Project, 1885-(1)
Prepared by Annie Ruth Davis
Place, Marion, S.C.
Date, July 14, 1937

No. Words_____8_____
Reduced from_____words
Rewritten by

HECTOR SMITH

Hold De Deal

I. Kitty, Kitty died O—O,
Kitty had a man.
Rather kiss a monkey,
Den to kiss a nigger man.
Hold de deal! Hold de deal!
I'm gwine to get drunk again.

II. Nigger on de horseback,
Thought he was de king.
Come along alligator,
En let de nigger in.
Hold de deal! Hold de deal!
I'm gwine to get drunk again.

Source: Hector Smith, age 79, ex-slave, Wahee section of Marion Co., S.C.
Personal interview, July 1937.

Code No.
Project, 1885-(1)
Prepared by Annie Ruth Davis
Place, Marion, S.C.
Date, July 14, 1937

No. Words_____9_____
Reduced from_____words
Rewritten by

HECTOR SMITH

Ex-Slave, 79 Years.

"I use to holler a heap in late years but after I lay it down, all dat leave me."

> Bulldogs a barkin,
> Howl! Howl!
> Bulldogs a barkin,
> Howl! Howl!
> Bulldogs a barkin,
> Howl! Howl!
> Ah—oodle—oodle—ou,
> Ah—oodle—oodle—ou,
> Ah—ou—ah—ou,
> Ah—oodle—ou,
> Ah—ou—ah—ou,
> Ah—oodle—oodle—ou.

Source: Hector Smith, 79 years, ex-slave, Wahee section of Marion Co., S.C.
Personal interview, July 1937.

Project 1885-(1)
Folk Lore
Spartanburg, S.C.
District No. 4
May 28, 1937.

Edited by:
R.V. Williams

JANE SMITH

Stories Of Ex-Slaves

"Aunt" Jane Smith, 80 years old, says that she was only eight years old when the war ended, and that her recollections are very meagre as to conditions during slavery.

Her mother belonged to John Snoddy, who owned a farm a few miles west of Spartanburg. Her father was owned by Dr. Miller of a nearby plantation. She stated that she was old enougth to rock the cradle for the white babies during slavery.

She stated that she could remember seeing some of the slaves being whipped on their bare backs with a plaited hickory stick, or thong. She never received any whippings. She said that a man once cut at her with his thong, but that she escaped the blow by dodging.

She said she remembered seeing a small child with a piece of bread in its hand when a hog entered the house and in snatching at the bread, caught the child's hand near the thumb with its tusks. When running off, the hog carried the child with it, dragging it along into the field. All the other children and some men ran after the hog and caught it. The other colored children were whipped, but by staying in the house and watching the babies, keeping them safe from other pigs which had also entered the house, she was not whipped.

Aunt Jane said that when the Yankee soldiers came to the house, they were just as thick as the "fingers on her hands." She held up her hands for inspection to illustrate how thick the soldiers stood in the ranks. She said they did not take anything, but that they crawled under the house to get the hen eggs. One soldier, she said, came to the house and asked if there were any horses on the farm. A colored woman told him that there were no horses on the place, but just at that time, one of the horses in a nearby stable neighed, and the soldier threatened the woman's life for lying to him. She says she doesn't remember whether the soldier took the horses but thinks that he did.

The soldiers told the colored people that they free, but she said that didn't signify much to her mind. Some time afterwards, she said her father came and carried her and her mother to his master's place. Later, she came to Spartanburg and got a job as a cook and washerwoman.

When asked if she knew anything about conjuring, she stated that she had heard of it but didn't know anything about it. When asked if she had ever seen a ghost, she said, "No, but I heard one once." She said that one night after her master had killed "hisself" in the barn with a pistol, she heard the doors being shut, the windows being slammed, and the chairs rocking on the front porch all by themselves. She declared that the wind was not blowing and that a "ghost was doing all dem things."

She stated that she had been married twice; had reared a houseful of children; had adopted some and reared them, but that she didn't have anybody to work for her now but "him," referring to her husband who was sitting on a trunk.

"Thank the Lord for coming to see me," she said, as the writer left.

>SOURCE: Jane Smith, Concord St., Spartanburg, S.C.
>Interviewer: F.S. DuPre

United States. Work Projects Administration

Project 1885-1
Folklore
Spartanburg, Dist. 4
Nov. 9, 1937

Edited by:
Elmer Turnage

MARY SMITH

Stories From Ex-Slaves

"I liked to went crazy when my brother, Bob, went to Arkansas. Den Marse George Young wrote our names in a book and give it to my ma. It was jes' a small mem'randum book. We kept it till Miss Addie, dat is Mrs. Billy, give ma de Bible storybook, and den she copied our names in dat one. De little book was about wore out den; so it was burned up when Miss Addie had done finished writing our names in de storybook. Us gwine to keep dat book and hand it down atter we done left dis earth. Ma been dead now over fifty years.

"I sho nu'sed Marse George's chilluns fer him, when I was a little gal. Jimmie, Willie, Conquest, Jack, Katie and Annie was Marse's chilluns. Conquest dead now. Marse George had a great big house. He was a jes'tice of de peace or something or 'nother den. I don't know what year my ma died, but Marse had her buried at New Chapel. Dat same year we raised a big crop of corn, cotton and peanuts, and had plenty hogs. Marse let us have all we wanted. He let us hang our meat in his smokehouse dat year.

"Befo' ma died and I was a little gal, a terrible thing happened to us. Across de Enoree on another place, de Miller place, Fannie Miller run away. Dey couldn't find her fer a long time. Dey told my marster to git her. One Sunday my ma got ready to dress me fer Sunday school. She bathed me and when she looked in de drawer she couldn't find my clothes. All of her clothes was gone, too. I cried 'cause I couldn't go to Sunday school. Maude, de woman what lived next to us, went to church. She saw Fannie dar wid all ma's clothes on. She told Marse about it and he sont out and had Fannie caught. She had come to our house and got de clothes on Saturday evening. She had dem hid in a old house on our place. Dey put her in jail, and den her marster come and whupped her and sont de clothes back to ma. She never tried to run off agin.

"Jack Gist, a slave of Gov. Gist, run away once and lived in a cave fer five months befo' de white folks found him. He went down on 'de forest' and dug a cave near de road in sight of de Harris Bridge which still spans de Fairforest Creek at dat p'int. De cave wasn't dug on Governor Gist's land, but on a place know'd den as de old Jackson place. In de mid hours of night Jack come to see his friends and dey give him things to eat. When dey got him he had a hog, two geese, some chickens and two middles of meat. Cose de hog and de middles was stole.

"One night he was crossing de Fairforest Creek on a foot-log and he met Anderson Gist, one of de Governor's slaves. Dey talked fer awhile. Next morning, Anderson come wid his marster to de cave whar Jack was. Dey took all his things on to de big house, and he was whupped and put back to work. Governor Gist and our marster was good to deir slaves and dey didn't punish 'em hard like some of 'em did. We had lots more den dan we has had ever since.

"I never went to de field till atter freedom come. Dey wasn't hard on us in de fields and I liked to work. We worked mostly from sun-up till it was too dark to work. Marster's youngest girl, Mary Jane Young, married Mr. Dave Lane. Dey didn't have a wedding.

"My grandpa was a African and he talked real funny. He was low, chunky, fat and real black. He went around a lot befo' he died. He was de father of my mother, Clora. Granny, his wife, was called 'Fender' and she died de first year of freedom. She was sold and lived on a neighboring plantation. We went to see her every Saturday. Ma would always take us to see her, and if we didn't git to go, she come to see us. We liked to go, and Marse always give us a pass. De patrollers watch us like a hawk, but we had our passes and we told dem if dey bothered us our marster would handle 'em. He would, too, 'cause dat was 'de law'. Granny Fender was good looking. She wore purty beads, earrings and bracelets, and wrapped her head up in a red cloth. Her eyes and teeth flashed and she was always jolly. Sometimes we stay all night, but most de time we come back home. When she come to see us she always stay all night. All de old folks had real religion den, and it kept 'em happy. Folks now are too fancy fer religion and it ain't real. I has real religion and nothing don't worry me. I feels happy all de time over it.

"My marster give my mother de spot of ground and de lumber fer our church which was named New Chapel. De second church is on de same spot. De first preaching was had under a oak tree, or arbor. Uncle Tony Murphy was de first preacher. He was my favorite of all de preachers. Marse read de Bible to us, but sometimes others read it to us, too. His son, Bud, dat was killed in de first battle, used to come to de quarters and read de Bible to us.

"Alex Hall was de minister dat immersed us all. We was all Methodists, but out dar dey baptized everybody in de Fairforest no matter what church dey went to. Dar was fifty people baptized de day dat I was. Milly Bethane made me a big white robe to be baptized in. When I got out I had a white dress to put on. Dey had a tent fer us to go in to change our clothes. We was baptized in de Fairforest jes' above de Harris Bridge. Everybody sung while we was going under de water. Some of 'em shouted, too. It took de earthquake to shake religion in my husband. He was Emanuel Gist, de first one.

"Dat night, de people was hollering and woke me up. My husband called me. 'What dat?' he 'low. 'I don't know,' I says. He got up and run out. Soon he come back home and he was shaking all over. He fell on de bed. When de chimney started to fall, I told him to git up. He said he was too scared to git up. I pulled him up and he was so scared dat he shook all over. I opened de door. He was too scared to stand up. Next day he couldn't work; so he went off. I looked fer him till way in de night. When he did come home, he was rejoicing. He was wid religion and he never give it up. Dat was on de night of de earthquake. You could hear people hollering fer miles around."

Source: Mary Smith (N, 84), Buffalo St., Union, S.C.
Interviewer: Caldwell Sims, Union, S.C. (9/14/37)

S-260-264-N
Project: #1885
Augustus Ladson
Charleston, S.C.

MR. PRINCE SMITH

Experiences Of An Ex-Slave On Wardmalaw Island Massa Wus Kind To Slaves

Prince Smith, a man who is said to be over a hundred years of age, has lived on Wardmalaw Island practically all of his life. His experiences during slavery are very interesting and true to life. An interview with him revealed the following:

"I was bo'n an' raise' on dis island and was only frum here when de Civil War had begun. W'en Fort Sumter wus fired on mossa carried seventy of us to Greenville, South Ca'lina on account of its montanous sections, which was believed would have prevented the Yankees invasion in regard to their hide-out." We stayed een Greenville nearly four years. Durin' dat time mossa planted his fa'm an' we wurk as if we wus right here.

"The Yankees had gunboats," he continued, "but dey didn' help dem atoll fur dey couldn' make any a'tack dat dis place is so unsuited fur water battles. But forest' battles wus fight on Beaufort Island and Port Royale. We een Greenville didn' know enyt'ing 'bout whut wus goin' on except what wus brought to us collud people by dose who wus sent to da town. Mossa didn' tell us eny ting. Fur almos' four 'ears we stayed een Greenville w'en suddenly one Chuesday mornin' bright an' early, Sheridan came into Greenville on horse backs en' order ebery body to sarrendar. Colonels an' Gen'rals came een de city widout de firin' of a gun. We stayed dere 'til harvestin' time by de orders of Master Osland Bailey who saw to it dat we wus given money as a share fur our wurk.

"Mossa's custom at de end of de week wus to give a dry peck o' corn which you had to grin' on Sat'day ebenin' w'en his wurk wus done. Only on Chris'mus he killed en give a piece o' meat. De driber did de distribution o' de ration. All young men wus given four quarts o' corn a week, while de grown men wus given six quarts. All of us could plant as much lan' as we wuld fur our own use. We could raise fowls. My master wus a gentleman, he treat all his slaves good. My fadder an' me wus his favorite.

"Some o' de slaves had to wurk on Sunday to finish dere week's wurk. If dey didn' de dribber who wus a Negro would give a lashin' varyin' frum fifteen to twenty five chops. Only high-class massas had Negro dribbters, de crackers had white overseers.

"Like odder slaves had to hide frum dere mastas to hab meetin', us could hab ours any night we want to even widout his consent. When masta went to town any o' his slaves could ax him to buy t'ings for dem een Cha'leston. When Jews en peddlers came with clothes an' gunger to sell, we as chillun would go to him an' ax fur money to buy whut we want.

"He had about four hund'ed acres of land which he divided in two half by a fence. One 'ear he would plant one an' let de cattles pasture on de oder. We could also raise hogs 'long wood his but had to change pasture w'en he did. De people on his plantation didn' hab any need to steal from him fur he didn' 'low us to want fur any thing.

"Dere wus three kinds of days wurk on de plantation: One is de whole tas', meanin' a whole han' or a person een his prime. He wus given two tas' fur dis day's wurk. A tas' carried frum twenty four to twenty five rows which wus thirty-five feet long en twenty five feet wide. De shree fourth han' wus given one whole tas' which consists of twelve rows. All de young chillun wus included in dis group. De half han' was de old slaves who did a half tas' for dere day's work. When it was time to pick cotton, de shree fourth han' had to pick thirty pound' an' de half han' twenty fur dere day's wurk. Dose who attended to the gin only include de three fourth han'.

"Massa had shree kinds o' punishment fur dose who disobeyed him. One wus de sweatbox. It wus made de height of de person an' no larger. Jus' large 'nough so de person woodn' hab to be squeezed in. De box is nailed an' een summer is put een de hot sun; een de winter it is put in de coldest, dampest place. De next is de Stock. Wood is nailed on floor with de person lyin' on his back wid hans an' feet tied wood a heavy weight on de chest. De shird is de Bilboa. You are place on a high scaffold fur so many hours an' if you don' try to keep a level head, you'll fall an you will surely hurt yourself if your neck isn't broken. Most o' de time dey were put dere so dey could break dere necks."

SOURCE

Information from an interview with Mr. Prince Smith, who is supposed to be over a hundred years of age, Wardmalaw Island, S.C.

Project 1885-1
Folklore
Spartanburg, Dist. 4
Nov. 29, 1937

Edited by:
Elmer Turnage

SILAS SMITH

Stories From Ex-Slaves

"Lawsey, honey chile, how does I know jes' when I was born. All sech as dat don't mean nothing to us old slave time darkies. De mis'tus say, 'Silas, you sho was thirteen years old when dat 'Federate War wound up! Dat's all I knows and dat's what I goes by. De white folks is worrying 'bout my age being in sech and sech a year and all de like of dat. No sech as dat don't worry Silas, kaise he sho don't give it no mind, dat I doesn't.

"Mis'tus call us all to set down on de side steps wid our hats in our hands. She read dat paper. When she git through, us still sets, kaise no writing never aggrevated us niggers way back dar. She wait a few minutes; den she 'low: 'It means dat you all is free, jes' as free as I is.' 'Dumpling Pie' jumped up and started crying. We all looked at him, kaise he was a fat lazy thing dat laid around like dumplings a-laying over kraut, and we axed him what he was crying for. He say, 'I ain't gwine to be no free nigger, kaise dat brings in de Issue, and I wants to keep my ma and pa, and what is I'm gwine to do widout Marse Dusey?'

"Dat woke us up. Didn't narry nigger on dat entire plantation know what to do widout his marster. It was de awfulest feeling dat everything in dem quarters laid down wid dat night, de new feeling dat day was free and never had no marster to tell dem what to do. You felt jes' like you had done strayed off a-fishing and got lost. It sho won't no fun to be free, kaise we never had nothing.

"Next morning Mis'tus low, 'Silas, I wants you to keep on being my house boy.' Dat sound de best to me of any news dat I had got. She hired me and I jes' kept on den as I had been gwine befo'. De quarters broke up, kaise Marse Dusey couldn't keep all dem niggers, so Mis'tus low'd. Marse was at de war and Mis'tus took things on.

"Dat left only a few in de quarter. In de meantime, carpetbaggers and scalawags had put devilment in some of dem ig'nant niggers and dey thought dat if dey leave, de U.S. gwine to give dem a plantation atter de war had ceased, and plenty mules to make dem rich, like quality white folks. So by dat time dey was a-raring to git moved off. But I stay on wid Miss Sallie, as I called her den.

"One dark, rainy cold day a stranger come riding up on a po' hoss and fetched a note of sorrow. Marse Dusey had done died somewhars, and Mis'tus was widowed to de ground. I stayed on, and in a year she died. Mr. Thomas Smith of Hickory Grove is de onliest chile living of my mis'tus, and he is 71 years old.

"Atter Mis'tus died, I went to live wid my pa on Mr. 'Baby' John Smith's place. He had been my pa's marster. Way back den it was so many John Smiths. 'Pears like it was mo' den dan now. Dat why dey call Mis'tus' husband 'John Dusey'. Each John had a frill to his name so dat folks could keep dem straight in deir minds whenever dey would speak of dem. Mis'tus sho was good to me. I 'members her chilluns' names well; Misses Aurita and Amenta. Miss Amenta married Mr. Sam Jeffries. Miss Rachael, Mis'tus other daughter, married Mr. John Morrow. Her 'Baby' John married a lady whose name I jes' disremembers, anyway dey had a son called 'Jeff'. He lived between Hickory Grove and Broad River. All dese Smiths which I gives you renumeration of is de Hickory Grove Smiths. You jes' has to keep dem straight yet."

    Source: Silas Smith (N, 85), Gaffney, S.C.
    Interviewer: Caldwell Sims, Union, S.C. (11/27/37)

United States. Work Projects Administration

Code No.
Project, 1885-(1)
Prepared by Annie Ruth Davis
Place, Marion, S.C.
Date, May 17, 1937

No. Words_____
Reduced from ____ words
Rewritten by

_____

JESSIE SPARROW

Ex-Slave, 83 years.

"Honey, my white folks been well-to-do peoples. Dey ain' been no poor white trash. Dey hab 'stonishing blood in dey vein. I been b'long to Massa Sam Stevenson wha' lib right down dere 'cross Ole Smith Swamp. Dey ain' hab no chillun dey own, but dey is raise uh poor white girl dere, Betty. Dey gi'e (give) she eve'yt'ing she ha'e en dey school she too."

"De ole man, he mind ain' been zactly right when he die. Dey say he bury some o' he money down dere on he place jes 'fore he die. Coase I dunno nuthin 'bout it, but dats wha' dey tell me. Dey say dey never is find dat money a'ter he been dead. Reckon it dere yet, I dunno. Peoples use'er aw de time be plough up kegs en box full o' money en va'uables wha' de well-to-do folks been hide dere."

"De white peoples use'er bury dey silver en dey money en aw dey va'uables late on uh evenin' er early on uh mornin' when de Yankees come 'bout. De Yankees 'stroy aw us white peoples va'uables wha' dey is see. Um—— dem Yankees sho' was 'structive whey dey is went."

"My ole mammy been Sally Stevenson 'fore she marry en den she wuz Sally Bowens. My ole Missus take she 'way from her mammy when she wuz jes uh little small girl en never wouldn't 'low her go in de colored settlement no more. She been raise up in de white folks house to be de house girl. Never didn't work none tall outside. She sleep on uh pallet right down by de Missus bed. She sleep dere so she kin keep de Missus kivver (cover) up aw t'rough de night. My mammy ain' never do nuthin but been de house girl. My Missus larnt (learned) she how to cut en sew so she been good uh seamstress is dere wuz anywhey. She help de Missus make aw de plantation clothes en dere ain' never been no better washer en ironer no whey den my ole mammy wuz."

"When I wuz uh little small girl, us lib right dere in my ole Missus yard. Dey le' us chillun play aw us wanna den. Never did hadder do none hard work tall. My Massa is some uh time send we chillun in de field to scare de crow offen de corn. Ain' never been no hoe hand in me life. When dey send we to scare de crow 'way, we is go in de field when fuss (first) sun up en we is stay dere aw day. Coase we is come to de house when 12 o'clock come en ge' we sumptin uh eat. Dese white folks 'round here don' hab no chillun to scare de crow offen dey corn nowadays. Dey has aw kind o' ole stick sot (set) 'bout in de field wid ole pant en coat flying 'bout on dem to scare de crow 'way. Dere be plenty crow 'bout nowadays too. I hears em hollerin aw 'bout in dis sky 'round 'bout here."

"I 'member when I use'er nu'se de white folks baby. I al'ays did lub to nu'se de babies, but I didn't never lub to nu'se no ug'y baby. I lub to hab uh pretty baby to nu'se. Didn't lak no boy baby neither. Don' lak boy baby nohow. Lubbed little girl baby. Lubbed to take de little girls en dress em up in dey pretty clothes en carry dem out under de trees to 'muse dem whey dere wuz plenty peoples 'bout to see em. Mammy al'ays 'ud fuss at me 'bout puttin' on dey best clothes, but I ain' never do lak dese nu'se do nowadays. I take care o' my babies, didn't never 'low em wallow in de dirt lak yunnah see dese nu'se do 'bout here dese day en time."

"I 'members one time I been nu'se little boy baby en I is larnt he hair to curl jes uz pretty. I bresh he hair eve'y morning en twist it 'round me finger en he is had pretty curl uz dere wuz anywhey. Never lak de Missus to cut my baby hair off neither when I had larnt it to curl."

"I been lub to wash little baby clothes too. I is primp em up so nice. Never did put no starch much in em. I do me best on em en when I ge' t'rough, dey been look too nice to le' de child muss up."

"Honey, I can' stand no chillun fuss 'round me no more dese days. Don' hab no chillun fuss 'round me peaceful little place. I tell aw me chillun en grandchillun en great-grandchillun dat I can' stand no chillun fuss 'round me no more. My Sammie, he marry three times en I ax him why he wanna marry so many time. I ain' never see no man I is wan' since my ole man die."

"I ain' wha' I use'er to be, child. I ain' able to do nuthin more now but dem little bit o' clothes wha' Miss Betty hab. Coase she clothes ain' hard to wash. Miss Betty mighty clean, honey, she mighty clean. She don' strip she bed but eve'y udder week en den de sheet ain' dirty one speck. She does wash she self eve'y day en de sheet don' ge' de crease out dem from one time dey wash till de next. I say I gwinna wash Miss Betty clothes jes uz long uz de Massa'll le' me em."

Source: Personal interview with Mom Jessie Sparrow, age 83, colored, Marion, S.C., May 1937.

Code No.
Project, 1885-(1)
Prepared by Annie Ruth Davis
Place, Marion, S.C.
Date. May 24, 1937

JESSIE SPARROW

Ex-Slave, 83 years.

"I dunno, child, I don' 'member nuthin more den I tell yuh de udder time. Is yuh been to see Maggie Black yet? I dunno how old she, but I know she been here. No, child, Maggie ain' dead. She lib right down dere next Bethel Church. She move 'way from Miss Mullins house when Gus die. Coase I ain' ne'er been in she house a'ter she move dere, but dey say she hab uh mighty restful place dere. Dat wha' dey tell me. Maggie oughta could tell yuh aw 'bout dem times. I ain' know nuthin more to tell yuh. Don' tell yuh aw I know."

"Who my mammy wuz? My mammy been Sallie Stevenson 'fore she marry en den a'ter she marry, she waz Sallie Bowens. Don' know whey dey ge' de Bowens from cause my pa been b'long to be uh Evans. Dat how come Miss Betty know so much 'bout me. She say we mighty nigh de same age. Coase I don' never 'spute Miss Betty word, but I don' t'ink so."

"No, child, I dunno. Dunno how many chillun my mammy is hab. Dey aw been die sech uh long time dat I don' forgot. Coase George, de carpenter, my brother. He been train up by uh good carpenter man en Henry, wha' paint aw dese house 'bout here, b'long to be annuder one uv we. It jes lak 'bout my own chillun, I ain' 'member how many dey wuz. I know dere 'bout t'ree uv dem big-guns dead, but aw dem babies, Lawd, I ain' 'member how many dere wuz. Can' never recollect nuthin 'bout how many dere been come here."

"My mammy been de house girl in my white folks house. She marry when she ain' but 13 year old. Dat wha' she tell me. She say she marry to ge' outer de big house. Dat how come she to marry so soon. Say de white folks take she way from she mammy when she won' but uh little small girl en make she sleep right dere on uh pallet in de Missus room aw de time 'fore she marry. Coase a'ter she marry, she been de house girl right on but she never stay in de Missus house when night come. Us chillun ain' been 'low to stay in de big house. Dey hab uh room put on de kitchen fa my mammy en she family to lib in. We chillun stay right dere in de yard whey my mammy could look a'ter us in en 'round. My mammy hadder stay 'bout my ole Missus aw de day en help she cut en sew de plantation clothes en wash en iron. Den she hadder help make quilts outer aw de scrap dat been left o'er a'ter de garment was cut out."

"Us chillun been fed from de table right dere in de Missus kitchen en some uv de time my mammy 'ud bring us sumptin to eat, wha' wuz cook in de Missus kitchen, en le' us eat it in she room. Dey'ud gi'e us hominy en milk en meat fa us break'ast. My white folks hadder uh lot uv cows en dey'ud gi'e us chillun plenty milk en clabber to eat. We is hab milk en clabber eve'y day en dey is gi'e us plenty meat to eat, so dey is dat. Child, I ain' know no slack eatin' 'round my ole Missus. Some uv de time we hab hoecake en den annuder time dey'ud gi'e us obben (oven) bread. Dey cook eve'yt'ing on de fireplace in dem days, eve't'ing. Jes hab rods put 'cross de fireplace in de kitchen wid pot hang on it. Dat whey dey cook us ration. Dey'ud gi'e us t'ings lak peas en collards en meat fa we dinner. Den dey'ud gi'e us uh big bowl uv corn bread en clabber late in de evenin' cause jes lak I is call to yuh jes now, dey is use milk right smart in dem days. I lak eve'yt'ing wha' dey is hab to eat den. Dey never eat lak dese peoples eats nowadays. I won' larnt to lak aw kind uv t'ing. Dey use'er cook poke salad wha' been season wid meat. Don' yuh know wha' dat? Poke salad is come up jes lak dose weed out dere en dey is cut de top offen dem en take aw de hard part outer em en den dey is boil em uh long time wid meat. Dey is eat right good too. Don' lak spinach en aw dat sumptin en don' lak celery neither. Don' lak butter put in nuthin I eats. I laks me squash fried down brown lak wid grease in de pan. I laks me beets wid uh little vinegay on em en season wid some sugar sprinkle on em. Don' lak em jes wid nuthin but uh little salt en butter smear aw o'er dem lak some uv dese peoples 'bout here eat em nowadays."

"Yas'um, we use'er eat plenty uv em possum. Eve'y one dey is ketch, us parent cook it. Us eat aw kinder wild animal den sech uz coon, possum, rabbit, squirrel en aw dat. Hab plenty uv fish in dem days too. Hab pond right next de white folks house en is ketch aw de fish dere dat we is wan'. Some uv de time dey'ud fry em en den some uv de time dey'ud make uh stew. Dey'ud put uh little salt en onion en grease in de stew en anyt'ing dey been ge' hold uv."

"Massa Sam been hab uh heap uv colored peoples 'sides we, but dey lib up on de hill in de quarters. My Missus, she see to it she self dat dey hab good bed wha' to sleep on en plenty sumptin uh eat. She docker (doctor) em when dey ge' sick too en she be mighty anxious ef dey sick mucha. Us hab good clothes en shoes den too. Coase de peoples'ud wear more clothes den, en dey'ud put on more undey shirt in de winter den dey wear in de summer. My white folks'ud make de plantation clothes outer gingham en jeanes cloth mostly. Dat jeanes cloth be wha' dey make little coat en pant outer. Dat sumptin jes lak homespun."

"No, child, dey ain' ne'er gi'e us no money den. Never need no money den. My Massa been provide eve't'ing us hab, honey, eve'yt'ing. We ain' lak fa nuthin den. We chillun ain' been big 'nough to do nuthin but scare de crow offen de corn en some uv de time my ole Missus'ud hab we chillun sweepin' outer in de yard when she be out dere wid us."

"Yas'um, honey, my white folks al'ays'ud see dat dey colored peoples'ud go to chu'ch (church) eve'y Sunday. We hadder walk dere to de white big Methodist Chu'ch up de road en sot en de gallery. Yas'um de white folks is stay down en we is go up. Ef we chillun never go, my ole Missus'ud teach us de catechism right dere in de back yard. Hadder wash us face en hand en come dere to she. Yas'um, I 'members dat aw right."

"My white folks'ud ride to chu'ch in dey big ole carriage en dey driver'ud hab dey big black hosses bresh jes uz shiny. I forge' de driver name. Dey hab uh pair uv dem black hosses wha' been match hosses en dey is look jes lak. En den one day de ole Yankees is come t'rough dere en dey is carry one uv dem 'way. A'ter dat dey hadder use one uv de plantation hoss in de place uv dis carriage hoss. De Missus'ud al'ays take my mammy in de carriage wid she too. Never left her home, so she tell me. Jes stuff she down dere 'tween de seats somewhey."

Source: Mom Jessie Sparrow, age 83, colored, Marion, S.C.
Personal interview, May 1937.

United States. Work Projects Administration

Code No.
Project No. 1885-(1)
Prepared by Annie Ruth Davis
Place, Marion, S.C.
Date, September 7, 1937

JESSIE SPARROW

Ex-Slave, 83 Years Marion, S.C.

"No, honey, dere ain' not a soul live here but me. Man stay in dat other room dere just to be a little bit of company for me when night come. He ain' not a speck of kin to me, not a speck. Oh, he pay me a little somethin, but it not much. Mostly, I does want him for protection like. Ain' got but just dis one room for myself cause dat part out dere does be just like out in de yard. Dis Miss Mary Watson house en she tell me stay on here dat de house ain' worth no fixin. Don' know how long I be here. No, honey, I ain' got no property only just myself. Ain' got not a bit. Ain' got nothin, child. I can' do no work dese days but dat little bit of washin dat Miss Betty have en dat ain' nothin to depend on. Just try to do a little somethin to help myself along. Nothin worth to speak bout though."

"Miss Betty say we bout one age. My daddy belonged to Miss Betty father en dat how-come she know dere ain' much difference in us age. My mammy was de house 'oman on old man Sam Stevenson plantation en dat whe'

I was born. When we was freed, I was a little small girl en my daddy moved us up here in town right over dere on de Gibson place. Fore den, when he have a mind to see us, he had to come cross de swamp dere to old man Sam Stevenson place en dat de reason he move us. He say it take too much pains to keep dat gwine back en forth. I remembers I finished growin right up here in dis town over dere on de Gibson place. My mammy have task to cook dere en my daddy been de butler man, but I was small den. Can' recollect much bout it. Reckon I wouldn' hardly know de place whe' I was born if I go back dere now. De old man Sam Stevenson had nice house, but it burn down long time back. Dey tell me dat de first court de peoples in Marion did ever know bout meet right dere on dat same spot. Coase I don' know nothin bout it, but dat what I hear dem say."

"My Massa had a big plantation, honey, a big plantation wid heap of colored people house. I remember dey call up dat way from de house on de hill en all de servants house set up dere. So I hear my mammy say she know bout some white folks dat didn' half feed dey colored people en didn' half clothe dem in de winter neither, but our white folks always treat us mighty good. Put shoes on all us feet in de winter en give us abundance of ration all de time."

"Honey, I hear dem talkin bout dat war, but I can' tell you nothin bout dat. I recollects I see dem Yankees when dey come through my Massa plantation en took his best carriage horse. Had two of dem big black carriage horses dat was match horses en dem Yankees carry one of dem away wid dem. I hear dem say de white folks would bury dey silver en money in pots en barrels to hide dem from de Yankees. Oh, dem fiddlin Yankees ax nobody nothin. Just go in de house en take dat what dey wanted. Go right in de house en plunder round en take de peoples best things. Wouldn' take no common things. Wasn' right, but dey done it. I hear talk dat a man plowed up a chest or somethin another de other day full of money, so dey tells me. I hear plenty peoples plow up all kind of things dese days in old fields dat ain' been broke up or throwed out for years. I hear so, but I know I ain' never found none though."

"I sho been here when dat shake come here, child. I been married ever since I was a grown 'oman en I was stayin right over yonder in dat house dere. My son Henry was de baby on me lap den en he tell me de other day dat he was bout 50 now. It come like a wind right from dat way. Some people tell me de ground was just a shakin en a mixin up, but I don' know how de ground was doin cause I never go on it. I hear de lumberation comin or dat what I calls it en it come long en hit de side of de house so hard dat all de dishes was just a rattlin. Every time de earth commence shakin, dem dish start jinglin. It come bout de early part of de night. I didn' know what to think it was till somebody come dere en say it been a earthquake. Say de ground was just a workin up. I tell you I ain' know what it was to be scared of, but dere been de old Ark (boarding house) standin cross de street den en dem people was scared most to death. Dey thought it was de Jedgment comin on. Reckon I would been scared worser den I was, but I didn' get on de ground. No, honey, I reckon de house dat was standin up in dat day en time was substantial like en it didn' worry none of dem."

"Is you seen Maggie Black any more? She been right

sick, but she better now. Yes, she been right puny. Don' know what ail her."

"Honey, what can you tell me bout dat white man dat been shoot up bout Mullins de other day. I hear people talk bout a man been shot by another man, but I ain' know nothin more den dat. Ain' hear none of de details only as dey tell me dey catch de man dat got away next Dillon tryin to get back home. I tell you it a bad place up dere in Mullins durin dis tobacco time. Dey tell me dere be such a stir up dat people be rob en shoot all bout dere. Dat de reason I stay back here whe' ain' nobody to worry me. Some of dem be seekin for you when you sleep en den another time dey get you when you gwine long de road. I don' like so much fuss en rousin en mix up round me. Dat de reason I does stay here by myself."

"De people just livin too fast dis day en time, honey. You know some of dese people, I mean my race, dey got a little bit of education en ain' got no manners. I tell dem if dey ain' got no manners, dey ain' got nothin cause manners carries people whe' a dollar won' carry you. Dis education don' do everybody no good. It get some of dem standin on de top of dey heads. Dat what it done to dem. Coase dey say everybody chillun got to go to school dis year en dat a good thing cause dere be so many runnin round makin mischief when dey ain' in school. I used to tell my chillun I buy dey book en satchel en keep plenty meat en bread for dem to eat en dey portion been to go dere en get dey learnin. If dey get whippin at school, I tell dem go back en get more. Didn' never entice dem to stay home."

"All I know bout Abraham Lincoln was dat he Abraham Lincoln en he de one cause freedom. I recollect dey used to sing song bout him, but I done forget it now. Say dey hung Abraham Lincoln on de sour apple tree or old Jeff Davis or somethin like dat. Honey, dat all I know. Can' recollect nothin more den dat bout it."

"Child, dis a pretty bad time de people got dese days, I tell you. Coase I thankful don' nobody worry me. All treats me nice, both white en black, what knows me. I be gwine down de street en folks come out de courthouse en say, 'Ain dat Mom Jessie? Mom Jessie, don' you remember me?' I say, 'I know your favor, but I can' call your name.' Dey tell me en laugh en let me lone. It just like dis, child, I puts my trust in de Lord en I lives mighty peaceful like. I ain' got a enemy in de world cause everybody speaks appreciatively of me. Dere somebody bringin me somethin to eat all de time en I don' be studyin bout it neither. First one en den de other bring me a plate en somethin another. Don' want me to do no cookin. Say I might fall in de fire. Honey, de lady come by here de other day en tell me I gwine get de old 'oman money pretty soon now dat dere been so much talk bout. I be thankful when it get here too, child, cause I wants to get first one thing en de other to do some fixin up bout my house."

"Well, honey, I tired now cause I ain' much today nohow. Can' recollect nothin else dis mornin. Don' know what you want to hear bout all dem things for nohow."

Source: Mom Jessie Sparrow, age 83, ex-slave, Bond Street,
Marion, S.C.—Third Report.

Personal interview by Annie Ruth Davis, Sept., 1937.

United States. Work Projects Administration

Code No.
Project, 1885-(1)
Prepared by Annie Ruth Davis
Place, Marion, S.C.
Date, December 7, 1937

JESSIE SPARROW

Ex-Slave, 83 Years

"No, I ain' cold. I settin in de sun. Miss Ida, she went by here just now en call at me bout de door been open en lettin dat cold wind blow in on my back wid all de fire gone out. I tell her, it ain' botherin me none, I been settin out in de sun. Well, I don' feel much to speak bout, child, but I knockin round somehow. Miss Ida, she bring me dis paper to study on. She does always be bringin me de Star cause she know dat I love to see de news of Marion. It right sad bout de Presbyterian preacher, but everybody got to die, I say. Right sad though. We hear dat church bell here de other evenin en we never know what it been tollin for. I holler over dere to Maggie house en ax her how-come de church bell tollin, but she couldn' tell me nothin bout it. Reckon some chillun had get hold of it, she say. I tell her, dat bell never been pull by no chillun cause I been hear death note in it. Yes, honey, de people sho gwine horne (grieve) after Dr. Holladay."

"I say, I doin very well myself en I thankful I ain'

down in de bed. Mighty thankful I ain' down in de bed en can set up en talk wid de people when dey comes to see me. I ain' been up dere on your street in a long time. Can' do much walkin dese days cause I ain' got no strength to speak bout. Ain' been up town dere in bout two months. Mr. Jervey ax John Evans what de matter dat I ain' been comin to de store to get my rations en John Evans tell him I been under de weather. Somehow another, dey all likes me up dere en when dey don' see me up town on Saturday, dey be axin bout me. Mr. Jervey, he come here de other day en bring me some tobacco en syrup en cheese en some of dem other things what he know dat I used to buy dere. He tell me dey all was wantin to see me back up dere again. I say, I can' go up dere cause I give way in my limbs en just comes right down whe' I don' have nothin to catch to. Got dis old stick here dat I balances myself on when I goes out round bout de house here. Cose I don' venture to steady myself no far ways on it."

"No, child, I ain' been up your way in a long time. I wash for Miss Betty all my best days, but I ain' been up to de house in many a mornin. Miss Betty like myself now, she old. I tell dem up dere to de house, de last time I talk wid dem, don' mind Miss Betty cause her mind ain' no good. I say, just gwine on en do what you got to do en let Miss Betty rest. You see, Miss Betty always would have her way en dis ain' no time to think bout breakin her neither. Cose I don' know nothin bout it, but Miss Betty say we bout one age."

"I reckon Miss Betty got plenty pecans dis year cause she does rake dem up by de tubfuls bout dis time of de year. I got my share of dem last year, but I ain' got no mind dat I gwine get any dis year less I go up dere. Yes, mam, I got my share last year cause when I went to carry Miss Betty washin home, I could pick up all I wanted while I come through under de trees. My Lord, Miss Betty, she had a quantity of dem last year, but I ain' hear what de crop doin dis year. I don' care though cause I wouldn' eat dem nohow widout I beat dem up en I ain' in no shape to go to all dat trouble. I loves peanuts good as anybody, but I couldn' never chew dem widout dey was beat up."

"Honey, my child en her daughter comin from de northern states dis Christmas to see me. Her name Evelyn, but dey call her Missie. She write here dat she want to come en I tell my Sammie to send word dey is welcome. Cose dey gwine stay wid my son, Sammie, cause dey got more room den I is en dey got a cookin stove, too, but she gwine be in en out here wid her old mammy off en on. Yes'um, I wants to see her mighty bad since it be dat she been gone from here so long. When she first went up dere, she worked for a white family dere to Hartford, Connecticut, but it won' long fore she got in a fidget to marry en she moved dere to Philadelphia. Dat whe' she livin now, so my Sammie tell me."

"Den dere another one of my chillun dat I say, I don' never 'spect to see no more on dis side of de world. Evelina, she get married en go way out west to live. She de one what used to nurse Lala up dere to Miss Owens' house. My God, honey, she been crazy bout Lala. Don' care what she been buy on a Saturday evenin, she would save some of it till Monday to carry to dat child. My Evelina, she always would eat en she used to bring Lala here wid her a heap of times to get somethin to eat. She would come in en fetch her dat tin plate up dere full of corn bread en molasses en den she would go to puttin dem ration way.

Would put her own mouth full en den she would cram some of it down Lala's mouth in de child's belly. You see, I always would keep a nice kind of syrup in de safe cause I don' like none dese kind of syrup much, but dis here ribbon cane syrup. My Lord, dat child would stand up dere en eat just as long as Evelina poke it down her. Oh, Lala been just a little thing plunderin bout en I tell Evelina dat she ought not to feed dat child dem coarse ration, but she say, 'Lala want some en I gwine give it to her cause I loves her.' No, child, Miss Owens never didn' worry her mind bout whe' Evelina been carry dat child. You see, she been put trust in Evelina."

"I don' know what to tell you, honey. I bout like Miss Betty now. My 'membrance short dese days. Oh, I hear talk bout all kind of signs de people used to worry over en some of dem still frets bout dem, too. Hear talk dat you mustn't wash none on de New Years' Day. It bad luck, so a heap of dem say. Den some folks say it a sign of death to hear a owl holler at night. Some people can' bear to hear dem, but don' no owls worry me, I say. Lord, Maggie, dis child ax me how a owl holler when it a sign of death. Well, dey does holler a right good space apart. Don' holler right regular. I ain' hear one holler now in a long time, but I used to hear dem be hollerin plenty times out dere somewhe' another in dem trees. Say, when some people been hear dem holler on a night, dey would stick a fire iron in de fire en dat would make de owl quit off. I hear talk bout a lot of people would do dat. Den dere another sign de people does have bout de New Years' Day. Reckon dat what dey call it, I don' know. No, mam, I don' understand nothin bout it, but I does hear people speak bout dey craves to get a cup of peas en a hunk of hog jowl on de first day of de year. Say, dem what put faith in dem kind of victuals on de New Years' Day, dey won' suffer for nothin no time all de next year. Cose I don' know, but I say dat I eats it cause I loves it."

"Well, child, dat bout all I know to speak bout dis evenin. It gettin so cold, I don' know whe' I can manage here much longer or no. Cose my Sammie, he want me to go stay dere wid him, but I can' stand no chillun fuss round me no more. I tell him dese people bout here be in en out to ax bout me right smart en I think bout I better stay here whe' dere ain' nobody to mind what I do. You see, honey, old people is troublesome en I don' want to be noways burdensome to nobody. Yes, mam, I gwine be right here waitin, if de Lord say so, de next time I see you makin up dat path."

> Source: Mom Jessie Sparrow, age 83, colored, Marion, S.C.
> Personal interview by Annie R. Davis, Dec., 1937.

United States. Work Projects Administration

Code No.
Project, 1885-(1)
Prepared by Annie Ruth Davis
Place, Marion, S.C.
Date, October 11, 1937

JESSIE SPARROW

Ex-Slave, 83 Years

"Good morning, honey, I ain' much today. How you is? No, I can' talk nothin bout dem times today. Ain' know no more den I done tell you. I doin very well considerin I can' get bout like I wants to. Doin very well, honey. Peoples mighty nice to me, white en black. Cose I don' venture to get far off de lot, I be so poorly dese days. Ain' been bout up town dere in a month since Saturday."

"Well, my chillun say for me to go live wid dem, but I don' want to go down to dat other far end of de town. I tell dem dey worry me so dat I think I rather be here in dis piece of house. See, I has such good neighbors bout me here en dere be so much a fightin en gwine on in dat other end of town. All de peoples speaks well of me, both white en black, of dem dat knows me. Yes, mam, Miss Ellen tell me fore she die for me to stay right here in dis house long as I live en ain' nobody is gwine worry me neither. No, child, Miss Mary Watson don' worry me, not one speck bout dis house. Miss Mary de only child dat Miss Ellen got left here. No, honey, I ain' studyin bout gwine nowhe' yet. Cose de house may fall down on me cause dat dere old kitchen over dere was good when I come here, but it rot down. Dat how-come I ain' got no stove. De kitchen rot down en de rain come in on de stove en rust it out. No, dey don' worry me none. I tell dem I ain' got nothin, but I settin here just as satisfied like. Cose I may get a little pension soon, but don' know when it gwine get here. I ain' hear tell of nobody gettin it yet. I tell lady dat come here if I get it, it be all right en if I don' get it, dat be all right too."

"Big sale on today, ain' dere, child? I hear talk bout dey gwine sell all de Witcover property en all dat, but I don' know. Dey sho got a pretty day for it. I had on my old thick sweater, but it too hot. I had to pull it off en put on dis here thin jacket. Can' go bout too naked, honey."

"Yes'um, I know it was you come here de other night. Cose I can' see so good, but I can hear de people voice en tell who dere time I hear dem comin up dat path. You see, I don' light my lamp first night nohow, dere be so much grass round here de mosquitoes comes in en worries me right smart."

"Miss Foxworth en dem fixin to plant dey turnips over dere. Miss Foxworth, I likes her very well to speak. She good-hearted, kind en clever. She comes over en talks wid me often cause us been friends ever since fore de old man been gone. Dey ain' got no kind of garden yet, but dey fixin to plant a fall garden out dere."

"No, child, I done put Miss Betty clothes down. Tell her I ain' able to wash no more en my Lord, Miss Betty sho hate to hear me say dat. Won' dat Miss Betty clothes was so hard, but it was de totin dem back en forth en den dere be so little bit of money in dem, didn' pay to hire nobody to carry dem. Cose she didn' pay me nothin worth much cause she didn' never have nothin much, but a little changin of underclothes en bout one dress. Just had to starch bout one petticoat en one dress, but I can' hardly wash for myself dese days en I wouldn' never venture to do hers no more. No, honey, my conscience wouldn' allow me to overpower Miss Betty for dem little bit of somethin en dey ain' dirty neither. You see, since Miss Emma been stayin dere, she in charge de house en uses all her tablecloths en such as dat. Miss Emma, she mighty nice to me. Every time I go up dere en I ain' been doin nothin for her neither, she see can she find a cup of fresh milk or somethin another to hand me."

"Reckon I gwine be lonesome right bout dis side next week cause all de colored schools gwine be open up Monday. You see, dere be so many school chillun en teacher livin on dis here street. Dat child over dere say she gwine be home right sharp after she be finish pickin cotton next week. I say I ain' be obliged to leave dis country cause my white folks wouldn' never venture to come dere to dat other end of town to see me. All dese chillun bout here mighty good to me. Don' never let me suffer for nothin. Dey caution me not to risk to cook nothin over dat fireplace cause dey say I might tumble over en can' catch myself. No, dey tell me don' do no cookin, I might fall in en burn up. No, child, I ain' chance to cook none on dat fireplace since I been sick. Different ones brings me somethin dis day en dat day. Don' suspicion nothin bout it till I see dem comin. Celeste over dere brings me breakfast en dinner every day en I don' never bother wid no supper cause I lays down too early. Den dey keeps me in plenty bread en rolls en I keeps a little syrup on hand en eats dat if I gets hungry. Dere Marguerite all de time bringin me somethin, if it ain' nothin but a pitcher of ice. You see, dey makes dey ice en it ain' costin her nothin. When I see her turn out dat piazza, I know she comin here. I ain' see her today, but I lookin for her. Used to wash for dem too. Honey, I done a lot of work bout dis town en I don' suffer for nothin. All de people bout here be good to me."

"No, mam, I ain' gwine let you take no more pictures. Ain' gwine take no more. If Miss Montgomery say she comin here to take more pictures, tell her I ain' gwine take no more. No, child, I ain' studyin bout no pictures. I don' want no more. I got one big one up dere on de wall dat show me en my mammy en my son, Sammie, settin in a automobile. Dat my picture settin up dere wid de white blouse on. I tell dem I look like somethin den, but I too old en broke up now. My daughter, she want a picture en she kept on after us till we went up dere to whe' de carnival was. Carnival man had a automobile dat he take your picture in en we get in en set down en he snap de picture. I tell dem dey got one now en dat ought to be sufficient. Dat my mammy settin dere by me. She was sho a fine lookin woman. Lord, Lord, honey, dem chillun love dem pictures, but I ain' studyin bout wantin my picture scatter all bout de country."

"Yes, child, I sleeps all right. Go to bed early too fore anybody else round here do. Yes, mam, I goes to bed early en don' never get up none till I see day shine in dem cracks. I was figurin somebody else ax me dat de other day. Believe it was Dr. Dibble. My Sammie, he a mammy child. He never stop till he send de doctor here to see could he find out de ailment dat seem like was eatin me way. Dr. Dibble come here en set down in dat chair en ax me a heap of questions. Den he test my blood en give me a tonic dat he say would hope me. Yes, mam, dat my Sammie doctor en he goes to see him often, he does have such a misery in his head. Dat de first time Dr. Dibble ever been here, but I likes he manner mighty well. Dr. Zack was a good doctor too. Cose dat what dey tell me, but I ain' know nothin bout it. No, child, I been healthy all my days en I ain' had to worry bout no doctor. I tells dem when I falls down, I won' last long cause I been hearty all my days."

"Your sister still in Dr. Dibble store (office), ain' she? Is she got a cook yet? Dat it, I glad she got somebody to depend on cause dese young people, can' tell bout dem. Dey be one place today en den dey apt to be another place de next day. I used to cook dere to lady house cross de street, but I never didn' cook no Sunday dinner dere. Dat lady been take in sewin en she would sew en press right on de big Sunday. I tell her dat a sin en she say she had to get finish somehow dat de folks was pushin her for dey clothes. I say, 'Well, dat you, ain' me.' I go dere on Sunday mornin en cook breakfast en clean up en put wood in de kitchen. Den I would go to church en left dem to cook what dinner dey get. Dat de reason I won' cook for none dese white folks dis day en time cause when dey pays you dat little bit of money, dey wants every bit your time. I been proud when dat lady move from here cause I was tired walkin de road back en forth. People come here en beg me to cook for dem, but I tell dem I gwine stay right here en do my bit of washin. Gwine get along somehow wid it."

"Bethel, down dere on de other side de jail, de only

church I ever been a member of. We got to fix us church twixt now en next year. It need fixin bad. You see, it right on de Main street gwine down en does be right public out to de people. I was fixin to go to church Sunday gone, but my child never come after me. My son, Sammie, never show up, but he come Sunday evenin laughin. Say, 'Ma, I know if I come by your house, you would want to go wid me.' No, I ain' been so I able to go in four Sundays."

"Child, you ought to had brought your parasol wid you cause you been settin here so long, you gwine be late gettin whe' you started. Dis here another hot day we got come here."

"Well, good-day, child. Speak bout how you is find Maggie Black to me when you pass back long dat street dere."

Source: Mom Jessie Sparrow, ex-slave, 83 years, Marion, S.C.
Personal interview by Annie Ruth Davis, October, 1937.

Project #1655
W.W. Dixon
Winnsboro, S.C.

ROSA STARKE

Ex-Slave 83 Years Old.

Rosa's grandfather was a slave of Solicitor Starke. Although she has had two husbands since slavery, she has thrown their names into the discard and goes by the name of Rosa Starke. She lives in a three-room frame house with her son, John Harrison, two miles south of Winnsboro, S.C., on the plantation of Mrs. Rebecca V. Woodward. She still does farm work, hoeing and picking cotton.

"They say I was six years old when de war commence poppin' in Charleston. Mammy and pappy say dat I was born on de Graham place, one of de nineteen plantations of my old marster, Nick Peay, in 1854. My pappy was name Bob and my mammy name Salina. They had b'longed to old Marse Tom Starke befo' old Marse Nick bought them. My brudders was name Bob and John. I had a sister name Carrie. They was all older than me.

"My marster, Nick Peay, had nineteen places, wid a overseer and slave quarters on every place. Folks dat knows will tell you, dis day, dat them nineteen plantations, in all, was twenty-seven thousand acres. He had a thousand slaves, more or less, too many to take a census of. Befo' de numerator git 'round, some more would be born or bought, and de nominator had to be sent 'round by Marse Nick, so old Miss Martha, our mistress, say. Her never could know just how many 'twas. Folks used to come to see her and ask how many they had and her say it was one of them sums in de 'rithmetic dat a body never could take a slate and pencil and find out de correct answer to.

"Her was a Adamson befo' her marry old marster, a grand big buckra. Had a grand manner; no patience wid poor white folks. They couldn't come in de front yard; they knowed to pass on by to de lot, hitch up deir hoss, and come knock on de kitchen door and make deir wants and wishes knowed to de butler.

"You wants me to tell 'bout what kind of house us niggers live in then? Well, it 'pend on de nigger and what him was doin'. Dere was just two classes to de white folks, buckra slave owners and poor white folks dat didn't own no slaves. Dere was more classes 'mongst de slaves. De fust class was de house servants. Dese was de butler, de maids, de nurses, chambermaids, and de cooks. De nex' class was de carriage drivers and de gardeners, de carpenters, de barber, and de stable men. Then come de nex' class de wheelwright, wagoners, blacksmiths and slave foremen. De nex' class I 'members was de cow men and de niggers dat have care of de dogs. All dese have good houses and never have to work hard or git a beatin'. Then come de cradlers of de wheat, de threshers, and de millers of de corn and de wheat, and de feeders of de cotton gin. De lowest class was de common field niggers. A house nigger man might swoop down and mate wid a field hand's good lookin' daughter, now and then, for pure love of her, but you never see a house gal lower herself by marryin' and matin' wid a common field-hand nigger. Dat offend de white folks, 'specially de young misses, who liked de business of match makin' and matin' of de young slaves.

"My young marsters was Marse Tom, Marse Nick, and Marse Austin. My young misses was Miss Martha, Miss Mary, and Miss Anne Eliza. I knows Marse Nick, Jr. marry a Cunningham of Liberty Hill. Marse Tom marry a Lyles and Marse Austin marry and move to Abbeville, after de war. Old marster die de year befo' de war, I think, 'cause my mammy and pappy fell in de division to Marse Nick and us leave de Graham place to go to de home place. It was called de Melrose place. And what a place dat was! 'Twas on a hill, overlookin' de place where de Longtown Presbyterian Church and cemetery is today. Dere was thirty rooms in it and a fish pond on top of it. A flower yard stretchin' clean down de hill to de big road, where de big gate, hangin' on big granite pillars, swung open to let de carriages, buggies, and wagons in and up to de house.

"Can I tell you some of de things dat was in dat house when de Yankees come? Golly no! Dat I can't, but I 'members some things dat would 'stonish you as it 'stonished them. They had Marseille carpets, linen table cloths, two silver candlesticks in every room, four wine decanters, four nut crackers, and two coffee pots, all of them silver. Silver castors for pepper, salt, and vinegar bottles. All de plates was china. Ninety-eight silver forks, knives, teaspoons and table-spoons. Four silver ladles, six silver sugar tongs, silver goblets, a silver mustard pot and two silver fruit stands. All de fireplaces had brass firedogs and marble mantelpieces. Dere was four oil paintin's in de hall; each cost, so Marse Nick say, one hundred dollars. One was his ma, one was his pa, one was his Uncle Austin and de other was of Colonel Lamar.

"De smoke-house had four rooms and a cellar. One room, every year, was filled wid brown sugar just shoveled in wid spades. In winter they would drive up a drove of hogs from each plantation, kill them, scald de hair off them, and pack de meat away in salt, and hang up de hams and shoulders 'round and 'bout de smokehouse. Most of de rum and wine was kep' in barrels, in de cellar, but dere was a closet in de house where whiskey and brandy was kep' for quick use. All back on de east side of de mansion was de garden and terraces, acres of sweet 'taters, water millions (watermelons) and strawberries and two long rows of beehives.

"Old marster die. De 'praisers of de State come and figure dat his mules, niggers, cows, hogs, and things was worth $200,000.00. Land and houses I disremember 'bout. They, anyhow, say de property was over a million dollars. They put a price of $1,600.00 on mammy and $1,800.00 on pappy. I 'member they say I was worth $400.00. Young Marse Nick tell us dat the personal property of de estate was 'praised at $288,168.78.[A]

"De Yankees come set all de cotton and de gin-house afire. Load up all de meat; take some of de sugar and shovel some over de yard; take all de wine, rum, and liquor; gut de house of all de silver and valuables, set it afire, and leave one thousand niggers cold and hongry, and our white folks in a misery they never has got over to de third generation of them. Some of them is de poorest white folks in dis State today. I weeps when I sees them so poor, but they is 'spectable yet, thank God.

"After de war I stuck to de Peay white folks, 'til I got married to Will Harrison. I can't say I love him, though he was de father of all my chillun. My pappy, you know, was a half white man. Maybe dat explain it. Anyhow, when he took de fever I sent for Dr. Gibson, 'tend him faithful but he die and I felt more like I was free, when I come back from de funeral, than I did when Marse Abe Lincoln set us free. My brudder, Bob, had done gone to Florida.

"I nex' marry, in a half-hearted way, John Pearson, to help take care of me and my three chillun, John, Bob, and Carrie. Him take pneumonia and die, and I never have a speck of heart to marry a colored man since. I just have a mind to wait for de proper sort, till I git to heaven, but dese adult teachers 'stroy dat hope. They read me dat dere is no marryin' in heaven. Well, well, dat'll be a great disappointment to some I knows, both white and black, and de ginger-cake women lak me.

"Is I got any more to tell you? Just dis: Dere was 365 windows and doors to Marse Nick Peay's house at Melrose, one for every day in de year, my mistress 'low. And dere was a peach tree in de orchard so grafted dat dat peach tree have ripe peaches on it in May, June, July, August, September, and October."

Project #1655
W.W. Dixon
Winnsboro, S.C.

JOSEPHINE STEWART

Ex-Slave 85 Years Old.

Phinie Stewart, as she is known in the community where she lives, is a small, black negress, who shows her age in appearance and movements. She lives with Robert Wood, a hundred yards back of the Presbyterian Church manse at Blackstock, S.C. Robert Wood married Phinie's niece, who is now deceased. Phinie has no property, and depends entirely on the charity of Robert Wood for her support.

"Does you know where de old Bell House is, about a mile de other side of Blackstock, on de Chester road? Yes? Well, dere is where I was borned, in May, 1853.

"I doesn't know who my pappy was. You know in them times folks wasn't particular 'bout marriage licenses and de preacher tying de knot and all dat kind of thing. But I does know mammy's name. Her name was Celie. Dese eyes of mine is dim but I can see her now, stooping over de wash tub and washing de white folks' clothes every Monday and Tuesday.

"Us belonged to Marster Charlie Bell and his lady, Miss Maggie Bell, our mistress in them slavery days.

Does I 'member who Miss Maggie was befo' her married Marster Charlie? Sure I does. Mistress was a daughter of Miss Anne Jane Neil, who lived to be a hundred and five years old, and its writ on her tombstone in Concord Cemetery. I 'spect you has seen it, ain't you? Old Miss Anne Neil was a Irish lady, born in Ireland across de ocean. She had a silver snuff box; I seen it. She'd take snuff out dat box, rub it up her nose and say: 'De Prince of Whales (Wales) give me dis box befo' I come to dis country, and I was presented to his ma, Queen Victoria, by de Duke of Wellington on my sixteenth birthday.' Old Miss Anne Neil claims she was born over dere de very night of de battle of Waterloo. And she would go on and 'low dat when de duke took her by de hand and led her up to de queen, him say: 'Your Majesty, dis young lady was born on de night of our great victory at Waterloo.'

"My young mistress was named Miss Margaret. She married Marse Wade Brice. I was give to them when I was 'bout five years old and I went along with them to Woodward, S.C. My mammy was give to them, too, at de same time. Us lived in Marse Wade's quarter, to de east of de white folks' house. Dere was a row of log houses, 'bout ten I think. Mammy and me lived in one dat had two rooms. De chimney was made of sticks and mud, but de floor was a good plank floor. De bed was a wood bedstead wid a wheat straw tick. Dere was no windows to de house, so it was warm in de winter time and blue blazing hot in de summer time.

"My white folks was mighty good to us; they fed us well. Us had wooden shoes and no clothes a-tall in de summer, 'cept a one-piece slip on. My mistress die 'bout a year after her marry, and then Marster Wade marry

Miss Tilda Watson, a perfect angel, if dere ever was one on dis red earth. She take a liking to me right at de jump, on first sight. I nussed all her chillun. They was Walter, Ida, Dickey, Lunsford, Wade, Mike, and Wilson. Then I nussed some of her grandchillun. Mr. Brice Waters in Columbia is one of them grandchillun.

"Marse Wade went off to de war and got shot in de hip, but he jined de calvary (cavalry) soon after and was away when de Yankees come through. De Yankees burned and stole everything on de place. They took off all de sheep, mules, and cows; killed all de hogs; cotch all de chickens, ducks and geese; and shot de turkeys and tied them to deir saddles as they left. De gin-house made de biggest blaze I ever has seen. Dere was short rations for all de white folks and niggers after dat day.

"In 1870 I was still dere wid Marse Wade and Miss Tilda, when de devil come along in de shape, form, and fashion of a man. He was name Simon Halleg. I was young then, and a fool, when I married dat no 'count nigger. Us had two chillun, a boy, Allen, and a girl, Louise. Louise sickened and died befo' she was grown. Allen married and had one child, but him and de child are dead. My husband run away and left us.

"About de time of de great cyclone, Miss Tatt Nicholson, a cousin of Miss Tilda, come down and took me to Chester, to be a maid at de Nicholson Hotel. I liked de work, but I got many a scare while I was dere. In them days every hotel had a bar where they would mix whiskey and lemons. Men could just walk up, put deir foots on de brass rail of de bar counter and order what they want, and pay fifteen cents a drink. Sometimes they would play cards all night in de bar. One night an old gent stopped his wagon, dat had four bales of cotton on it, befo' de hotel. He come in to get a drink, saw a game going on and took a hand. Befo' bed time he had lost all his money and de four bales of cotton outside.

"No, I didn't work in slavery times. Chillun didn't have to work. De only thing I 'members doing was minding de flies off de table wid a brush made out of peacock tail-feathers.

"All de slaves had to go to church at Concord twice every month and learn de Shorter Catechism. I has one of them books now, dat I used seventy-five years ago. Want to see it? (She exhibits catechism printed in 1840 for slaves.)

"I left de hotel and come back to Miss Tilda Brice. I married Jacob Stewart then, and he was a good man. Us had no chillun. He been gone to glory eight years, bless God.

"Yes, sir, I 'members de earthquake. It set a heap of people to praying dat night. Even de cows and chickens got excited. I thought de end of de world had come. I jined de Red Hill Baptist Church then, but my membership is now at de Cross Roads Baptist Church. Brother Wright, de pastor, comes to see me, as I'm too feeble to gallivant so far to church.

"Dis house b'longs to Joe Rice. My nephew rents from him and is good enough, though a poor man, to take care of me.

"Please do all you can to get de good President, de Governor, or somebody to hasten up my old age pension dat I'm praying for."

Project 1885-1
FOLKLORE
Spartanburg Dist. 4
May 24, 1937

Edited by:
Elmer Turnage

BETTIE SUBER

Stories From Ex-Slaves

"I was born near old Bush River Baptist Church in Newberry County, S.C. This was the white folks' church, but the colored folks have a Bush River church in that section now. I was grown when the war started. I was a slave of Bonny Floyd. He was a good man who owned several slaves and a big farm. I was the house-girl then, and waited on the table and helped around the house. I was always told to go to the white folks' church and sit in the gallery.

"When the Patrollers was started there, they never did bother Mr. Bonny's slaves. He never had any trouble with them, for his slaves never run away from him.

"The Ku Klux never come to our place, and I don't remember seeing them in that section.

"We took our wheat to Singley's Mill on Bush River to be ground. We made all our flour and grain. We plowed with horses and mules.

"I am an old woman, sick in bed and can't talk good; but glad to tell you anything I can."

Source: Bettie Suber (96), Newberry, S.C.
Interviewer: G.L. Summer, Newberry, S.C. (5/18/37).

Project 1885-1
FOLKLORE
Spartanburg, S.C.
May 25, 1937

Edited by:
Elmer Turnage

ELLEN SWINDLER

Stories From Ex-Slaves

"I was born on the Enoree River in Newberry County. Tom Price was my master. I married Nathan Swindler when I was about grown. My father and mother was Dave and Lucy Coleman. I had a brother and several sisters. We children had to work around the home of our master 'till we was old enough to work in de fields, den we would hoe and pick cotton, and do any kinds of field work. We didn't have much clothes, just one dress and a pair of shoes at a time, and maybe one change. I married in a ole silk striped dress dat I got from my mistress, Miss Sligh. We had no 'big-to-do' at our wedding, just married at home. In cold weather, I had sometimes, heavy homespun or outing dress. When Saturday afternoons come, we got off from work and do what we want. Some of us washed for de week. We had no schools and couldn't read and write. Sometimes we could play in our yards after work was over or on Saturday afternoons. On Christmas the master give us something good to eat. We didn't have doctors much, but de ole folks had cures for sickness. Dey made cherry-bark tea for chills and fever, and root-herb teas for fevers. Lots of chills and fevers then. To cure a boil or wart, we would take a hair from the tail of a horse and tie it tight around both sides of the sore place. I think Abe Lincoln was a great man, and Jeff Davis was a good man too. I think Booker Washington was a great man for de colored race. I like it better now than de way it was in slavery time."

    Source: Ellen Swindler (78), Newberry. S.C. Interviewed by:
    G.L. Summer, Newberry, S.C., May 20, 1937.

Project #1655
W.W. Dixon,
Winnsboro, S.C.

MACK TAYLOR

Ex-Slave 97 Years.

Mack Taylor lives six miles southeast of Ridgeway, S.C., on his farm of ninety-seven acres. The house, in which he resides, is a frame house containing six rooms, all on one floor. His son, Charley, lives with him. Charley is married and has a small family.

"Howdy do sir! I sees you a good deal goin' backwards and forwards to Columbia. I has to set way back in de bus and you sets up to de front. I can't ketch you to speak to you, as you is out and gone befo' I can lay hold of you. But, as Brer Fox 'lowed to Brer Rabbit, when he ketched him wid a tar baby at a spring, 'I is got you now.'

"I's been wantin' to ask you 'bout dis old age pension. I's been to Winnsboro to see 'bout it. Some nice white ladies took my name and ask me some questions, but dat seem to be de last of it. Reckon I gwine to get anything?

"Well, I's been here mighty nigh a hundred years, and just 'cause I pinched and saved and didn't throw my money away on liquor, or put it into de palms of every Jezabel hussy dat slant her eye at me, ain't no valuable reason why them dat did dat way and 'joyed deirselves can get de pension and me can't get de pension. 'Tain't fair! No, sir. If I had a knowed way back yonder, fifty years ago, what I knows now, I might of gallavanted 'round a little more wid de shemales than I did. What you think 'bout it?

"You say I's forgittin' dat religion must be thought about? Well, I can read de Bible a little bit. Don't it say: 'What you sow you sure to reap?' Yes, sir. Us niggers was fetched here 'ginst our taste. Us fell de forests for corn, wheat, oats, and cotton; drained de swamps for rice; built de dirt roads and de railroads; and us old ones is got a fair right to our part of de pension.

"My marster, in slavery times, lived on de Wateree River. He had a large plantation and, I heard them say, four hundred slaves. He was a hard marster and had me whipped as many times as I got fingers and toes. I started workin' in de field when I was a boy fifteen years old. De work I done was choppin' de grass out of de cotton and pickin' de cotton. What's become of them old army worms dat had horns, dat us chillun was so scared of while pickin' cotton? I never see them dese days but I'd rather have them than dis boll weevil I's pestered wid.

"My marster's name was Tom Clark. My mistress was a gentle lady, but field niggers never got to speak to her. All I can say is dat de house slaves say she was mighty good to them. I saw de chillun of de white folks often and was glad they would play wid us colored chillun. What deir names? Dere was Marse Alley, Marse Ovid, Marse Hilliard, and Miss Lucy.

"Old marster got kilt in de last year of de war, and Miss Margaret, dat was our Mistress, run de place wid overseers dat would thrash you for all sorts of things. If they ketch you leanin' on your hoe handle, they'd beat you; step out of your task a minute or speak to a girl, they'd beat you. Oh, it was hell when de overseers was around and de mistress nor none of de young marsters was dere to protect you. Us was fed good, but not clothed so good in de winter time.

"My pappy didn't b'long to de Clarks at de commencement of de war. Old marster done sold him, 'way from us, to Col. Tom Taylor in Columbia. After de war, he run a shoe repair shop in Columbia many years befo' he died. His name was Douglas Taylor and dat is de reason I took de name, Mack Taylor, when I give in my name to de Freedman's Bureau, and I's stuck to it ever since.

"I members de Yankees. Not many of them come to Miss Margaret's place. Them dat did, took pity on her and did nothing but eat, feed deir horses, and gallop away.

"Us was never pestered by de Ku Klux, but I was given a warnin' once, to watch my step and vote right. I watched my step and didn't vote a-tall, dat year.

"Mr. Franklin J. Moses was runnin' for governor. Colored preachers was preachin' dat he was de Moses to lead de Negroes out of de wilderness of corn bread and fat grease into de land of white bread and New Orleans molasses. De preachers sure got up de excitement 'mongst de colored women folks. They 'vised them to have nothin' to do wid deir husbands if they didn't go to de 'lection box and vote for Moses. I didn't go, and my wife wouldn't sleep wid me for six months. I had no chillun by her. She died in 1874. After Nancy die, I marry Belle Dawkins. De chillun us had was George, Charley, Maggie and Tommy. Then Belle died, and I married Hannah Cunningham. Us had no chillun. After she died, I marry a widow, Fannie Goings, and us had no chillun.

"My son, George, is in Washington. My daughter, Maggie, is dead. Tommy was in Ohio de last I heard from him. I is livin' wid my son, Charley, on my farm. My grandson, Mack, is a grown boy and de main staff I lean on as I climb up to de hundred mile post of age.

"I b'longs to de Rehovah Baptist Church. I have laid away four wives in deir graves. I have no notion of marryin' any more. Goodness and mercy have followed me all de days of my life, and I will soon take up dis old body and dwell in de house of de Lord forevermore."

Project #1655
W.W. Dixon
Winnsboro, S.C.

DELIA THOMPSON
Ex-Slave 88 Years Old.

"I's heard tell of you, and sent for you to come to see me. Look lak I can no more git 'bout on dese under pins lak I use to. Dere's de swing you can set in or chair right by me, now which you rather? I's glad you takes de chair, 'cause I can keep steady gaze more better on dat face of your'n. Lord! I been here in dis world a long time, so I has. Was born on de Kilgo place near Liberty Hill, don't know what county 'tis, but heard it am over twenty-five miles from dis town.

"My old marster name Jesse Kilgo, so he was, and Mistress Letha Kilgo, dats his wife, good to him, good to me, good to everybody. My young mistress name Catherine, when her marry Marster Watt Wardlaw, I was give to them for a housemaid, 'cause I was trim and light complected lak you see I is dis very day a setting right here, and talking wid you. 'Members how 'twas young missie say: 'You come go in my room Delia, I wants to see if I can put up wid you'. I goes in dat room, winter time mind you, and Miss Charlotte set down befo' de fire, cook one of them pretty foots on de dog, don't you ketch dat wrong, dat it was a lap dog which 'twasn't but one of de fire-dogs. Some persons calls them andy irons (andiron) but I sticks to my raisin' and say fire-dogs. Well, she allowed to me, 'Delia, put kettle water on de fire'. So I does in a jiffy. Her next command was: 'Would you please be so kind as to sweep and tidy up de room'? All time turnin' dat lovely head of her'n lak a bird a buildin' her nest, so it was. I do all dat, then she say: 'You is goin' to make maid, a good one!' She give a silvery giggle and say: 'I just had you put on dat water for to see if you was goin' to make any slop. No, No! You didn't spill a drop, you ain't goin' to make no sloppy maid, you just fine.' Then her call her mother in. 'See how pretty Delia's made dis room, look at them curtains, draw back just right, observe de pitcher, and de towels on de rack of de washstand, my I'm proud of her!' She give old mistress a hug and a kiss, and thank her for de present, dat present was me. De happiness of dat minute is on me to dis day.

"My pappy name Isom then, but when freedom come he adds on Hammond. His pappy was a white man, and no poor white trash neither. My mammy name Viny. Us live in a log house close up in de back yard, and most all time I was in de big house waiting on de white folks.

"Did us git any 'ligion told us? Well, it was dis way, mistress talk heap to us 'bout de Lord, but marster talk a heap to us 'bout de devil. 'Twist and 'tween them, 'spect us heard most everything 'bout heaven and all 'bout de devil.

"Yankees dat come to our house was gentleman, they never took a thing, but left provisions for our women folks from their commissary.

"My first husband was Cupid Benjamin. My white

folks give me a white dress, and they got de white Baptist preacher, Mr. Collins to do de grand act for us. Cupid turned out to be a preacher. Us had three chillun and every night us had family worship at home. I's been no common nigger all my life; why, when a child I set up and rock my doll just lak white chillun, and course it was a rag doll, but what of dat. Couldn't I name her for de Virgin Mary, and wouldn't dat name cover and glorify de rags? Sure it would! Then I 'sociate wid white folks all slavery time, marry a man of God and when he die, I marry another, Tom Thompson, a colored Baptist preacher. You see dat house yonder? Dats where my daughter and grandchillun live. They is colored aristocracy of de town, but they has a mighty plain name, its just Smith. I grieve over it off and on, a kind of thorn in de flesh, my husband used to say. But both my husbands dead and I sets here twice a widow, and I wonders how 'twill be when I go home up yonder 'bove them white thunder heads us can see right now. Which one them men you reckon I'll see first? Well, if it be dat way, 'spect I'll just want to see Cupid first, 'cause he was de only one I had chillun by, and them his grandchillun out yonder."

Project #1655
W.W. Dixon
Winnsboro, S.C.

ROBERT TOATLEY

Ex-Slave 82 Years Old.

Robert Toatley lives with his daughter, his son, his son's wife, and their six children, near White Oak, seven miles north of Winnsboro, S.C. Robert owns the four-room frame house and farm containing 235 acres. He has been prosperous up from slavery, until the boll weevil made its appearance on his farm and the depression came on the country at large, in 1929. He has been compelled to mortgage his home but is now coming forward again, having reduced the mortgage to a negligible balance, which he expects to liquidate with the present 1937 crop of cotton.

Robert is one of the full blooded Negroes of pure African descent. His face, in repose, possesses a kind of majesty that one would expect in beholding a chief of an African tribe.

"I was born on de 'Lizabeth Mobley place. Us always called it 'Cedar Shades'. Dere was a half mile of cedars on both sides of de road leading to de fine house dat our white folks lived in. My birthday was May 15, 1855. My mistress was a daughter of Dr. John Glover. My master married her when her was twelve years old. Her first child, Sam, got to be a doctor, and they sho' did look lak brother and sister. When her oldest child, Sam, come back from college, he fetched a classmate, Jim Carlisle, wid him. I played marbles wid them. Dat boy, Jim, made his mark, got 'ligion, and went to de top of a college in Spartanburg. Marse Sam study to be a doctor. He start to practice and then he marry Miss Lizzie Rice down in Barnwell. Mistress give me to them and I went wid them and stayed 'til freedom.

"My childhood was a happy one, a playin' and a rompin' wid de white chillun. My master was rich. Slaves lived in quarters, 300 yards from de big house. A street run through the quarters, homes on each side. Beds was homemade. Mattresses made of wheat straw. Bed covers was quilts and counter-panes, all made by slave women.

"My mammy's pappy was a slave brick-mason, b'longin' to a white family named Partillo, from Warrington, Virginia. He couldn't be bought 'less you bought his wife and three chillun wid him.

"Never had any money; didn't know what it was. Mammy was a house woman, and I got just what de white chillun got to eat, only a little bit later, in de kitchen. Dere was fifty or sixty other little niggers on de place. Want to know how they was fed? Well, it was lak dis: You've seen pig troughs, side by side, in a big lot? After all de grown niggers eat and git out de way, scraps and everything eatable was put in them troughs; sometimes buttermilk poured on de mess and sometimes potlicker. Then de cook blowed a cow horn. Quick as lightnin' a passle of fifty or sixty little niggers run out de plum bushes, from under de sheds and houses, and from everywhere. Each one take his place, and souse his hands in de mixture and eat just lak you see pigs shovin' 'round slop troughs. I see dat sight many times in my dreams, old as I is, eighty-two years last Saturday.

"'Twas not 'til de year of '66 dat we got 'liable info'mation and felt free to go where us pleased to go. Most of de niggers left but mammy stayed on and cooked for Dr. Sam and de white folks.

"Bad white folks comed and got bad niggers started. Soon things got wrong and de devil took a hand in de mess. Out of it come to de top, de carpetbag, de scalawags and then de Ku Klux. Night rider come by and drap something at your door and say: 'I'll just leave you something for dinner'. Then ride off in a gallop. When you open de sack, what you reckon in dere? Liable to be one thing, liable to be another. One time it was six nigger heads dat was left at de door. Was it at my house door? Oh, no! It was at de door of a nigger too active in politics. Old Congressman Wallace sent Yankee troops, three miles long, down here. Lot of white folks was put in jail.

"I married Emma Greer in 1879; she been dead two years. Us lived husband and wife 56 years, bless God. Us raised ten chillun; all is doin' well. One is in Winnsboro, one in Chester, one in Rock Hill, one in Charlotte, one in Chesterfield, one in New York and two wid me on de farm near White Oak, which I own. I has 28 grandchillun. All us Presbyterians. Can read but can't write. Our slaves was told if ever they learned to write they'd lose de hand or arm they wrote wid.

"What 'bout whuppin's? Plenty of it. De biggest whuppin' I ever heard tell of was when they had a trial of several slave men for sellin' liquor at da spring, durin' preachin', on Sunday. De trial come off at de church 'bout a month later. They was convicted, and de order of de court was: Edmund to receive 100 lashes; Sam and Andy each 125 lashes and Frank and Abram 75 lashes. All to be given on deir bare backs and rumps, well laid on wid strap. If de courts would sentence like dat dese days dere'd be more 'tention to de law.

"You ask me 'bout Mr. Lincoln. I knowed two men who split rails side by side wid him. They was Mr. McBride Smith and Mr. David Pink. Poor white people 'round in slavery time had a hard tine, and dese was two of them.

"My white folks, de Mobleys, made us work on Sunday sometime, wid de fodder, and when de plowin' git behind. They mighty neighborly to rich neighbors but didn't have much time for poor buckra. I tell you poor white men have poor chance to rise, make sump'n and be sump'n, befo' de old war. Some of dese same poor buckra done had a chance since then and they way up in 'G' now. They mighty nigh run de county and town of Winnsboro, plum mighty nigh it, I tell you. It makes me sad, on de other side, to see quality folks befo' de war, a wanderin' 'round in rags and tatters and deir chillun beggin' bread.

"Well, I mus' be goin', but befo' I goes I want to tell you I 'members your ma, Miss Sallie Woodward. Your grandpa was de closest neighbor and fust cousin to Dr. Sam. Deir chillun used to visit. Your ma come down and spen' de day one time. She was 'bout ten dat day and she and de chillun make me rig up some harness for de billy goat and hitch him to a toy wagon. I can just see dat goat runnin' away, them little chillun fallin' out backside de wagon and your ma laughin' and a cryin' 'bout de same time. I picks her up out de weeds and briars."

Project 1885-1
FOLKLORE
Spartanburg Dist. 4
May 25, 1937

Edited by:
Elmer Turnage

MARY VEALS

Slavery Reminiscences

"I was born in the town of Newberry, S.C. I do not remember slavery time, but I have heard my father and mother talk about it. They were Washington and Polly Holloway, and belonged to Judge J.B. O'Neall. They lived about 3 miles west of town, near Bush River. An old colored man lived nearby. His name was Harry O'Neall, and everybody said he was a miser and saved up his money and buried it near the O'Neall spring. Somebody dug around there but never found any money. There were two springs, one was called 'horse spring', but the one where the money was supposed to be buried had a big tree by it.

"I married Sam Veals, in 'gravel town' of Newberry. I had a brother, Riley, and some sisters.

"We would eat fish, rabbits, 'possums and squirrels which folks caught or killed. We used to travel most by foot, going sometimes ten miles to any place. We walked to school, three or four miles, every day when I was teaching school after the war. I was taught mostly at home, by Miss Sallie O'Neall, a daughter of Judge J.B. O'Neall.

"My father and mother used to go to the white folks' church, in slavery time. After the war colored churches started. The first one in our section was Brush Harbor. Simon Miller was a fine colored preacher who preached in Brush Harbor on Vandalusah Spring Hill. Isaac Cook was a good preacher. We used to sing, 'Gimme dat good ole-time religion'; 'I'm going to serve God until I die' and 'I am glad salvation is free'.

"Saturday afternoons we had 'off' and could work for ourselves. At marriages, we had frolics and big dinners. Some of the games were: rope jumping; hide and seek, and, ring around the roses. Of course, there were more games.

"Some of the old folks used to see ghosts, but I never did see any.

"Cures were made with herbs such as, peach tree leaves, boiled as a tea and drunk for fevers. Rabbit tobacco (life everlasting) was used for colds. Small boys would chew and smoke it, as did some of the old folks.

"I have seven children, all grown; fourteen grand-children, and several great-grand-children.

"Judge O'Neall was one of the best men and best masters in the country that I knew of. I think Abraham Lincoln was a good man, according to what I have heard about him. Jeff Davis was the same. Booker Washington was a great man to his country and served the colored race.

"I joined the church because I believe the bible is true, and according to what it says, the righteous are the only people God is pleased with. Without holiness no man shall see God."

Source: Mary Veals (72), Newberry, S.C. Interviewed by: G.L. Summer, Newberry, S.C. May 20, 1937.

Project 1885-1
Folklore
Spartanburg, Dist. 4
Oct. 21, 1937

Edited by:
Elmer Turnage

MARY VEALS
Stories From Ex-Slaves

"I don't own no house. I live in a rented house. Yes, I work fer my living. I don't 'member much 'bout slavery except what I heard my daddy and mammy say. My pa was Washing Holloway and my ma was Polly Holloway. Dey belonged to Judge O'Neall, and lived at his place 'bout three miles from town, near Bush River.

"Judge O'Neall's house was real old, and dey had a store near it called Springfield, a kind of suburb at dat time.

"After de war, we didn't have much clothes, 'cause everything was so high. Judge O'Neall died befo' de war was over, and his wife went to Mississippi to live wid her married daughter. After de war, Miss Sallie, who was Judge O'Neall's daughter, learn't me to read and write, and other things in books.

"My father and mother went to de white folks' church

in slavery time. After de war, de negroes built deir first church and called it a 'brush arbor'. A negro preacher named Simon Miller was a good man and done lots of good when he preached in de brush arbor. Dis was on de old Banduslian Springs hill, near de south fork of Scotts Creek."

    Source: Mary Veals (73), Newberry, S.C.
    Interviewer: G.L. Summer, Newberry, S.C. (9/30/37).

Project #1655
W.W. Dixon
Winnsboro, S.C.

MANDA WALKER

Ex-Slave 80 Years Old.

Manda Walker lives with her son-in-law, Albert Cooper, in a three-room frame cottage in Winnsboro, S.C. Albert's first wife was her daughter, Sallie. Five of their children and Albert's second wife, Sadie, occupy the house with Albert and Manda.

"Does you know where Horse Crick (Creek) branch is, and where Wateree Crick is? Ever been 'long de public road 'tween them water courses? Well, on de sunrise side of dat road, up on a hill, was where my slavery time marster live.

"I was born in de yard, back of de white folks' house, in a little log house wid a dirt floor and a stick and mud chimney to one end of de house. My marster was name Marse Tom Rowe and my mistress name Missy Jane Rowe. They de ones dat tell me, long time ago, dat I was born befo' de war, in 1857. Deir chillun was Miss Mary and Miss Miami.

"I no work much 'til de end of de war. Then I pick cotton and peas and shell corn and peas. Most of de time I play and sometime be maid to my young misses. Both growed into pretty buxom ladies. Miss Miami was a handsome buxom woman; her marry Marse Tom Johnson and live, after de war, near Wateree Church.

"My pappy name Jeff and b'long to Marse Joe Woodward. He live on a plantation 'cross de other side of Wateree Crick. My mammy name Phoebe. Pappy have to git a pass to come to see mammy, befo' de war. Sometime dat crick git up over de bank and I, to dis day, 'members one time pappy come in all wet and drenched wid water. Him had made de mule swim de crick. Him stayed over his leave dat was writ on de pass. Patarollers (patrollers) come ask for de pass. They say: 'De time done out, nigger.' Pappy try to explain but they pay no 'tention to him. Tied him up, pulled down his breeches, and whupped him right befo' mammy and us chillun. I shudder, to dis day, to think of it. Marse Tom and Miss Jane heard de hollerin' of us all and come to de place they was whuppin' him and beg them, in de name of God, to stop, dat de crick was still up and dangerous to cross, and dat they would make it all right wid pappy's marster. They say of pappy: 'Jeff swim 'cross, let him git de mule and swim back.' They make pappy git on de mule and follow him down to de crick and watch him swim dat swif' muddy crick to de other side. I often think dat de system of patarollers and bloodhounds did more to bring on de war and de wrath of de Lord than anything else. Why de good white folks put up wid them poor white trash patarollers I never can see or understand. You never see classy white buckra men a paterrollin'. It was always some low-down white men, dat never owned a nigger in deir life, doin' de patarollin' and a strippin' de clothes off men, lak pappy, right befo' de wives and chillun and beatin' de blood out of him. No, sir, good white men never dirty deir hands and souls in sich work of de devil as dat.

"Mammy had nine chillun. All dead 'cept Oliver. Him still down dere wid de Duke Power Company people, I think. When I come sixteen years old, lak all gals dat age, I commence to think 'bout de boys, and de boys, I 'spects, commence to take notice of me. You look lak you is surprised I say dat. You is just puttin' on. Old and solemn as you is, a settin' dere a writin', I bets a whole lot of de same foolishness have run through your head lak it run through Jerry's, when he took to goin' wid me, back in 1873. Now ain't it so?

"Us chillun felt de pivations (privations) of de war. Us went in rags and was often hungry. Food got scarce wid de white folks, so much had to be given up for de army. De white folks have to give up coffee and tea. De slaves just eat corn-bread, mush, 'taters and buttermilk. Even de peas was commanded for de army. Us git meat just once a week, and then a mighty little of dat. I never got a whuppin' and mammy never did git a whuppin'.

"Us all went to Wateree Presbyterian Church on Sunday to hear Mr. Douglas preach. Had two sermons and a picnic dinner on de ground 'tween de sermons. Dat was a great day for de slaves. What de white folks lef' on de ground de slaves had a right to, and us sure enjoy de remains and bless de Lord for it. Main things he preached and prayed for, was a success in de end of de war, so mammy would explain to us when us 'semble 'round de fireside befo' us go to bed. Her sure was a Christian and make us all kneel down and say two prayers befo' us git in bed. De last one was:

'Now I lay me down to sleep,
I pray de Lord my soul to keep.
If I should die befo' I wake,
I pray de Lord my soul to take.
Bless pappy, bless mammy,
Bless marster, bless missie,
And bless me. Amen!'

"Wheeler's men was just as hard and wolfish as de Yankees. They say de Yankees was close behind them and they just as well take things as to leave all for de Yankees. 'Spect dat was true, for de Yankees come nex' day and took de rest of de hog meat, flour, and cows. Had us to run down and ketch de chickens for them. They search de house for money, watches, rings, and silverware. Took everything they found, but they didn't set de house afire. Dere was just 'bout five of them prowlin' 'round 'way from de main army, a foragin', they say.

"When Miss Margaret marry, old marster sold out and leave de county. Us move to Mr. Wade Rawls' and work for him from 1876 to Jerry's death. Is I told you dat I marry Jerry? Well, I picked out Jerry Walker from a baker's dozen of boys, hot footin' it 'bout mammy's door step, and us never had a cross word all our lives. Us had nine chillun. Us moved 'round from pillar to post, always needy but always happy. Seem lak us never could save anything on his $7.06 a month and a peck of meal and three pounds of meat a week.

"When de chillun come on, us try rentin' a farm and got our supplies on a crop lien, twenty-five percent on de cash price of de supplies and paid in cotton in de fall. After de last bale was sold, every year, him come home wid de same sick smile and de same sad tale: 'Well, Mandy, as usual, I settled up and it was—'Naught is naught and figger is a figger, all for de white man and none for de nigger.'

"De grave and de resurrection will put everything all right, but I have a instinct dat God'll make it all right over and up yonder and dat all our 'flictions will, in de long run, turn out to our 'ternal welfare and happiness."

Project #1655
W.W. Dixon
Winnsboro, S.C.

NED WALKER

Ex-Slave 83 Years Old.

Ned Walker lives in the village of White Oak, near Winnsboro, S.C., in a two-room frame house, the dwelling of his son-in-law, Leander Heath, who married his daughter, Nora. Ned is too old to do any work of a remunerative character but looks after the garden and chickens of his daughter and son-in-law. He is a frequent visitor to Winnsboro, S.C. He brings chickens and garden produce, to sell in the town and the Winnsboro Hill's village. He is tall, thin, and straight, with kind eyes. Being one of the old Gaillard Negroes, transplanted from the Santee section of Berkeley County, in the Low Country, to the red hills of Fairfield County, in the Up Country, he still retains words and phrases characteristic of the Negro in the lower part of South Carolina.

"Yes sir, I's tall and slim lak a saplin'; maybe dat a good reason I live so long. Doctor say lean people lives longer than fat people.

"I hear daddy read one time from de Bible 'bout a man havin' strength of years in his right hand and honor and riches in his left hand, but whenever I open dat left hand dere is nothin' in it. 'Spect dat promise is comin' tho', when de old age pension money gits down here from Washington. When you 'spect it is comin'? De palm of my hand sho' begin to itch for dat greenback money. So you think it's on de way? Well, thank God for dat but it seem 'most too good to be true. Now I'll quit askin' questions and just set here and smoke and answer, whilst you do de puttin' down on de paper.

"Yes sir, I was born right here in de southeast corner of Winnsboro, on de Clifton place. De day I was born, it b'long to my master, David Gaillard. Miss Louisa, dats Master David's wife, 'low to me one day, 'Ned don't you ever call de master, old master, and don't you ever think of me as old miss'. I promise her dat I keep dat always in mind, and I ain't gonna change, though she done gone on to heaven and is in de choir a singin' and a singin' them chants dat her could pipe so pretty at St. Johns, in Winnsboro. You see they was 'Piscopalians. Dere was no hard shell Baptist and no soft shell Methodist in deir make up. It was all glory, big glory, glory in de very highest rung of Jacob's ladder, wid our white folks.

"Well, how I is ramblin'. You see dere was Master David and Mistress Louisa, de king bee and de queen bee. They had a plantation down on de Santee, in de Low Country, somewhere 'bout Moncks Corner. One day Master David buy a 1,385 acres on Wateree Creek. He also buy de Clifton place, to live in, in Winnsboro. I can't git my mind back to tell you what I wants for you to put on de paper. 'Scuse me, forgit everything, 'til you git my pedigree down.

"I done name Master David and Mistress Louisa. Now for de chillun. Us was told to front de boys name wid

Marse and de young ladies name wid Miss. Now us can go and git somewhere.

"Well, dere was Miss Elizabeth; she marry Mr. Dwight. Miss Maria marry another Mr. Dwight. Miss Kate marry Mr. Bob Ellison, a sheriff. Her got two chillun in Columbia, Marse David and Marse DuBose Ellison. Then for de boys; they all went to de war. Marse Alley got kilt. Marse Dick rise to be a captain and after de war marry Congressman Boyce's daughter, Miss Fannie. Marse Ike marry and live in de Low Country; he die 'bout two years ago. Marse Sam marry a Miss DuBose and went wid General Wade Hampton.

"Marse Sam's son cut a canal that divide half and half de western part of de whole world. Us niggers was powerful scared, 'til Marse David Gailliard took a hold of de business. Why us scared? Why us fear dat de center of de backbone of de world down dere, when cut, would tipple over lak de halfs of a watermelon and everybody would go under de water in de ocean. How could Marse David prevent it? Us niggers of de Gaillard generation have confidence in de Gaillard race and us willin' to sink or swim wid them in whatever they do. Young Marse David propped de sides of de world up all right, down dere, and they name a big part of dat canal, Gaillard Cut, so they did. (Gaillard Cut, Panama Canal)

"Well, I keep a ramblin'. Will I ever git to Marse Henry, de one dat looked after and cared for slaves of de family most and best? Marse Henry marry a Miss White in Charleston. He rise to be captain and adjutant of de fightin' 6th Regiment. After de war him fix it so de slaves stay altogether, on dat 1,385 acres and buy de place, as common tenants, on de 'stallment plan. He send word for de head of each family to come to Winnsboro; us have to have names and register. Marse Henry command; us obey. Dat was a great day. My daddy already had his name, Tom. He was de driver of de buggy, de carriage, and one of de wagons, in slavery. Marse Henry wrote him a name on a slip and say: 'Tom as you have never walked much, I name you Walker.'

"It wasn't long befo' daddy, who was de only one dat could read and write, ride down to Columbia and come back wid a 'mission in his pocket from de 'Publican Governor, to be Justice of de Peace.

"Marse Henry ladle out some 'golliwhopshus' names dat day. Such as: Caesar Harrison, Edward Cades and Louis Brevard. He say, 'Louis, I give you de name of a judge. Dan, I give you a Roman name, Pompey.' Pompey turned out to be a preacher and I see your grandpa, Marse William Woodward, in de graveyard when Uncle Pompey preached de funeral of old Uncle Wash Moore. Tell you 'bout dat if I has time.

"Well, he give Uncle Sam de name of Shadrock. When he reach Uncle Aleck, he 'low: 'I adds to your name Aleck, two fine names, a preacher's and a scholar's, Porter Ramsey.' 'Bout dat time a little runt elbow and butt his way right up to de front and say: 'Marse Henry, Marse Henry! I wants a big bulldozin' name.' Marse Henry look at him and say: 'You little shrimp, take dis then.' And Marse Henry write on de slip of paper: Mendoza J. Fernandez, and read it out loud. De little runt laugh mighty pleased and some of them Fernandezes 'round here to dis day.

"My mammy name Bess, my granddaddy name June,

grandmamny, Renah, but all my brothers dead. My sisters Clerissie and Phibbie am still livin'. Us was born in a two-story frame house, chimney in de middle, four rooms down stairs and four up stairs. Dere was four families livin' in it. Dese was de town domestics of master. Him have another residence on de plantation and a set of domestics, but my daddy was de coachman for both places.

"De Gaillard quarters was a little town laid out wid streets wide 'nough for a wagon to pass thru. Houses was on each side of de street. A well and church was in de center of de town. Dere was a gin-house, barns, stables, cowpen and a big bell on top of a high pole at de barn gate. Dere was a big trough at de well, kept full of water day and night, in case of fire and to water de stock. Us had peg beds, wheat straw mattress and rag pillows. Cotton was too valuable.

"Master didn't 'low de chillun to be worked. He feed slaves on 'tatoes, rice, corn pone, hominy, fried meat, 'lasses, shorts, turnips, collards, and string beans. Us had pumpkin pie on Sunday. No butter, no sweet milk but us got blabber and buttermilk.

"Oh, then, I 'bout to forgit. Dere was a big hall wid spinnin' wheels in it, where thread was spin. Dat thread was hauled to Winnsboro and brought to de Clifton place in Winnsboro, to de weave house. Dat house set 'bout where de Winnsboro Mill is now. Mammy was head of de weave house force and see to de cloth. Dere was a dye-room down dere too. They use red earth sometime and sometime walnut stain. My mammy learn all dis from a white lady, Miss Spurrier, dat Master David put in charge dere at de first. How long she stay? I disremembers dat.

Us no want for clothes summer or winter. Had wooden bottom shoes, two pair in a year.

"Mr. Sam Johnson was de overseer. Dere was 'bout 700 slaves in de Gaillard quarter and twenty in town, countin' de chillun. De young white marsters break de law when they teach daddy to read and write. Marse Dick say: 'To hell wid de law, I got to have somebody dat can read and write 'mong de servants.' My daddy was his valet. He put de boys to bed, put on deir shoes and brush them off, and all dat kind of 'tention.

"De church was called Springvale. After freedom, by a vote, de members jines up, out of respect to de family, wid de Afican Methodist 'Piscopalian Church, so as to have as much of de form, widout de substance of them chants, of de master's church.

"No sir, us had no mulattoes on de place. Everybody decent and happy. They give us two days durin' Christmas for celebratin' and dancin'.

"I marry Sylvin Field, a gal on de General Bratton Canaan place. Us have three chillun. Nora Heath, dat I'm now livin' wid, at White Oak, Bessie Lew, in Tennessee, and Susannah, who is dead.

"What I think of Abe Lincoln? Dat was a mighty man of de Lord. What I think of Jeff Davis? He all right, 'cordin' to his education, just lak my white folks. What I think of Mr. Roosevelt? Oh, Man! Dat's our papa.

"Go off! I's blabbed 'nough. You 'bliged to hear 'bout dat funeral? Will I pester you for 'nother cigarette? No sir! I ain't gonna smoke it lak you smoke it. Supposin' us was settin' here smokin' them de same? A Gaillard come up them steps and see us. He say: 'Shame on dat white man', turn his back and walk back down. A Woodward come up them steps and see us. He say: 'You d— nigger! What's all dis?' Take me by de collar, boot me down them steps, and come back and have it out wid you. Dat's 'bout de difference of de up and low country buckra.

"Now 'bout Uncle Wash's funeral. Uncle Wash was de blacksmith in de forks of de road 'cross de railroad from Concord Church. He was a powerful man! Him use de hammer and tongs for all de people miles and miles 'round. Him jine de Springvale Afican Methodist 'Piscopalian Church, but fell from grace. Him covet a hog of Marse Walt Brice and was sent to de penitentiary for two years, 'bout dat hog. Him contacted consumption down dere and come home. His chest was all sunk in and his ribs full of rheumatism. Him soon went to bed and died. Him was buried on top of de hill, in de pines just north of Woodward. Uncle Pompey preached de funeral. White folks was dere. Marse William was dere, and his nephew, de Attorney General of Arizona. Uncle Pompey took his text 'bout Paul and Silas layin' in jail and dat it was not 'ternally against a church member to go to jail. Him dwell on de life of labor and bravery, in tacklin' kickin' hosses and mules. How him sharpen de dull plow points and make de corn and cotton grow, to feed and clothe de hungry and naked. He look up thru de pine tree tops and say: 'I see Jacob's ladder. Brother Wash is climbin' dat ladder. Him is half way up. Ah! Brudders and sisters, pray, while I preach dat he enter in them pearly gates. I see them gates open. Brother Wash done reach de topmost rung in dat ladder. Let us sing wid a shout, dat blessed hymn, 'Dere is a Fountain Filled Wid Blood'.' Wid de first verse de women got to hollerin' and wid de second', Uncle Pompey say:

'De dyin' thief I see him dere to welcome Brother Wash in paradise. Thank God! Brother Wash done washed as white as snow and landed safe forever more.'

"Dat Attorney General turn up his coat in de November wind and say; 'I'll be damn! Marse William smile and 'low: 'Oh Tom! Don't be too hard on them. 'Member He will have mercy on them, dat have mercy on others'."

Project #1655
Stiles M. Scruggs
Columbia, S.C.

DANIEL WARING
Ex-Slave 88 Years Old.

"I was born in Fairfield County, South Carolina, in 1849, and my parents, Tobias and Becky Waring was slaves of the Waring family, and the Bookters and Warings was kin folks. When I was just a little shaver I was told I b'longed to the family of the late Colonel Edward Bookter of upper Fairfield County.

"The Bookter plantation was a big one, with pastures for cattle, hogs and sheep; big field of cotton, corn and wheat, and 'bout a dozen Negro families livin' on it, mostly out of sight from the Bookter's big house. Two women and three or four Negro chillun work there, preparin' the food and carin' for the stock. I was one of the chillun. Colonel Bookter's household had three boys; one bigger than me and two not quite as big as me. We play together, drive up the cows together, and carry on in friendly fashion all the time. The nigger chillun eat with the two black women in a place fixed for them off from the kitchen, after the white folks finish. We generally have same food and drink that the white folks have.

"When I was 'bout eleven years old my master took

me to Columbia one Saturday afternoon, and while Colonel Bookter was 'round at a livery stable on Assembly Street, he give me some money and tell me I could stroll 'round a while. I did, and soon find myself with 'bout a dozen of Master Hampton's boys. As we walk 'long Gervais Street, we met a big fine lookin' man with a fishin' tackle, goin' towards the river, and several other white folks was with him. As we turn the corner, the big man kinda grin and say to us: 'Whose niggers are you?' The bigger boy with us say: 'We all b'longs to Master Hampton.' He laugh some more and then reach in his pocket and give each one of us a nickel, sayin' to the white folks: 'Blest if I know my own niggers, anymore'.

"Yes sir, I was 'bout fourteen years old when President Lincoln set us all free in 1863. The war was still goin' on and I'm tellin' you right when I say that my folks and friends round me did not regard freedom as a unmixed blessin'.

"We didn't know where to go or what to do, and so we stayed right where we was, and there wasn't much difference to our livin', 'cause we had always had a plenty to eat and wear. I 'member my mammy tellin' me that food was gittin' scarce, and any black folks beginnin' to scratch for themselves would suffer, if they take their foot in their hand and ramble 'bout the land lak a wolf.

"As a slave on the plantation of Colonel Edward Bookter, I had a pretty good time. I knows I has work to do and I does it, and I always has plenty to eat and wear in winter and summer. If I get sick I has a doctor, so we set tight until 1865. After the war we come to Columbia, and mammy made us a livin' by washin' for white folks and doin' other jobs in the kitchen, and I worked at odd jobs, too.

"We didn't get much money from the Freedmen's outfit, which was 'stablished in Columbia. The white men who set it up and administered the Freedmen's funds and rations let some of their pets have much of it, while others got little or nothin'. An' existence become increasin' harder as nigger got more and more in the saddle.

"During the war, and it seem to me it would never end, we heard much 'bout President Lincoln. Niggers seem to think he was foolish to get into war, but they generally give him credit for directin' it right as far as he could. President Davis was powerful popular at the beginnin' of the conflict, but his popularity was far less when the war is over and he is in jail.

"I was 'most grown at the end of the war, and I was at no time popular with the black leaders and their white friends who rule the roost in Columbia for 'most thirteen years. I went back to my white friends in Fairfield County and work for years for Mister T.S. Brice, and others on the plantation.

"I has been married three times, and am now livin' with my third wife. She and me am makin' a sort of livin', and is yet able to work. I can only do de lightest work and the sweetest thought I has these days is the memory of my white friends when I was young and happy."

United States. Work Projects Administration

Code No.
Project, 1885-(1)
Prepared by Annie Ruth Davis
Place, Marion, S.C.
Date, June 2, 1937

NANCY WASHINGTON

Ex-Slave, 104 years.

"Come in child. Jes set right dere in dat chair whey I c'n be mindful uv yuh cause I ain' hear but sorta hard lak dese days. I jes come in outer de field whey I been chopping 'round uh little wid me hoe, but eve't'ing is grow so black 'fore me eye dat I t'ink I better rest meself uh little. I tries to help Sam (her son) aw I c'n, but I ain' mucha 'count no more. I 104 year old en I ain' gwinna be heah much longer. Me mark done strak (strike) me right dere dis a'ternoon. Dat been jes de way my ole mammy waz call."

"Does yah know whey dat place call Ash Pole? Dat whey I wuz raise up when I b'long to Massa Giles Evanson. He wuz uh good ole fellow. I ain' know wha' it wuz to ge' no bad treatment by my white people. Dey tell me some uv de colored peoples lib mighty rough in dat day en time but I ne'er know nuthin 'bout dat. I 'member dey is spank we chillun wid shingle but dey ne'er didn't hit my mudder."

"My Massa ne'er hab so mucha colored peoples lak

some uv dem udder white folks hab. Jes hab my mudder en eight head uv we chillun. Hab 'nough to gi'e eve'yone uv he daughter uh servant apiece when dey ge' marry. Ne'er hab nuthin but women colored peoples. My Massa say he ain' wan' no man colored peoples."

"De preacher Ford, wha' use'er lib right up dere in town, papa hab uh big ole plantation wha' been jes lak uh little town. He hab hundred colored peoples en dey is hab eve't'ing dere. Hab dey preachin' right dere on de plantation en aw dat."

"Coase my white folks hab uh nice plantation en dey keep uh nice house aw de time. I wuz de house girl dere en de one wha' dey'ud hab to wait on de Missus. Dey'ud carry me eve'ywhey dey go. Al'ays know how I wuz faring. My Missus wuz big en independent lak. Talk lak she mad aw de time, but she warnt. She ne'er wear no cotton 'bout dere no time. Hab her silk on eve'y day en dem long yellow ear bob dat'ud be tetchin right long side she shoulder. I al'ays look a'ter de Missus en she chillun. Wash dey feet en comb dey hair en put de chillun to bed. But child, some white folks is queer 'bout t'ings. Dey watch yuh gwine 'bout yuh work en den dey'll wan' yuh to do sumptin fa dem. De ole man take me 'way from helping de Missus en send me out to plow corn en drap peas. I wuz shame too cause I ne'er lak fa he to treat my Missus dat uh way."

"De peoples ne'er didn't cook in no stove den neither. Dey hab big ole round dirt ubben (oven) to cook dey ration in. Dey make dey ubben outer white clay en hadder build uh shelter over it cause dey'ud cook outer in de yard. Dey ne'er cook but jes twice uh week. Cook on Wednesday en den ne'er cook no more till Saturday. I 'member de big ole ham dat dey cook en de tatoes en so mucha bread. Jes hab 'bundance aw de time. I got uh piece uv de ole slavery time ubben heah now. I ge' it outer en show it to yuh. Dis is one uv de leads (lids) en dey'ud put uh chain en hook on dere en hang it up in de fireplace. Dat de way dey cook dey ration. O Lawd, ef I could ge' back to my ole home whey I could look in en see jes one more time, jes one more time, child."

"I wuz jes uh girl when de Yankees come t'rough dere. Dey look jes lak uh big blue cloud comin' down dat road en we chillun wuz scared uv em. Dat land 'round 'bout dere wuz full uv dem Yankees marchin' en gwine on. Dey ne'er bother my white folks but in some uv de places dey jes ruint eve't'ing. Burnt up en tore down aw 'bout dere."

"Yuh ain' ne'er see nobody weave no cloth nowadays. In de winter dey use'er al'ays put woolen on de little chillun to keep em from getting burnt up. Peoples wuz easy to cotch uh fire in dat time. Dey hab plenty uv sheep den en dis jes 'bout de time uv de year dat dey shear de sheep. Al'ays'ud shear de sheep in de month uv May. Dey is make aw kinder nice cloth den. I c'n charge en spin en make any kinder streak yuh wan'. Coase my mudder use'er weave de jeanes cloth en blanketing."

"Dey use'er hab some uv dem corn-shucking 'bout dere but I ne'er take no part in none uv dat. A'ter freedom declare, us pull boxes en dip turpentine. Dat wha' wuz in de style den."

"I won' but 'bout 16 when I marry en I hab uh nice wedding. Marry right dere in my Massa yard en hab white swass dress to wear. I marry uh settled man offen uh rich man plantation en dey ne'er wan' me to marry, but dey ne'er say nuthin 'gainst it. Dey hab good manners den en manners de t'ing dat carry peoples t'rough anyt'ing, child."

>Source: Nancy Washington, age 104, colored, Dusty Hills,
> Marion, S.C. (Personal interview, May 1937).

Project #1655
W.W. Dixon
Winnsboro, S.C.

CHARLEY WATSON
Ex-Slave 87 Years Old.

"Dis is a mighty hot day I tells you, and after climbing them steps I just got to fan myself befo' I give answer to your questions. You got any 'bacco I could chaw and a place to spit? Dis old darkie maybe answer more better if he be allowed to be placed lak dat at de beginnin' of de 'sperience.

"Where was I born? Why right dere on de Hog Fork Place, thought everybody knowed dat! It was de home place of my old Marster Daniel Hall, one of de Rockefellers of his day and generation, I tells you, he sho was. My pappy had big name, my marster call him Denmore, my mammy went by de name of Mariyer. She was bought out of a drove from Virginny long befo' de war. They both b'long to old marster and bless God live on de same place in a little log house. Let's see; my brother Bill is one, he livin' at de stone quarry at Salisbury, North Carolina. My sister Lugenie marry a Boulware nigger and they tells me dat woman done take dat nigger and make sumpin' out of him. They owns their own automobile and livin' in Cleveland, Ohio.

"Us live in quarters, two string of houses a quarter mile long and just de width of a wagon road betwixt them. How many slaves marster had? Dere was four hundred in 1850, dat was de year I was born, so allowing for de natural 'crease, 'spect dere was good many more when freedom come. Our beds was made of poles and hay or straw. Was my marster rich? How come he wasn't? Didn't he have a Florida plantation and a Georgia plantation? Didn't us niggers work hard for our vittles and clothes? It make me laugh de way de niggers talk 'bout eight hours a day. Us worked by de 'can and de can't system'. What way dat you ask me? Well, was dis way; in de mornin' when it git so you can see, you got to go to work and at night when it git so dark you can't see you ceasted to work. You see what I mean? My marster's white overseer 'dopted de 'can and can't system' of work hours. My mammy had to plow same as a man, she did sir. Sometimes they pulled fodder and fooled wid it on Sunday.

"You is a pushin' me a little too fast. Let me gum dis 'bacco and spit and I can do and say more 'zackly what you expect from me. My marster had sheep, goats, mules, horses, stallion, jackass, cows and hogs, and then he had a gin, tan yard, spinnin' rooms, weave room, blacksmith shop and shoe shop. Dere was wild turkeys on de place, deer in de cane brakes and shad in de Catawba River. De Indians fetch their pots and jars to sell, and peddlers come to big house wid their humps on their backs and bright yards of calico and sich things de missus lak to feel and s'lect from. I see money then, but I never see a nigger wid money in his paws in slavery time, never!

"Us was fed good on corn meal, hog meat, milk, butter, 'lasses, turnips, beans, peas and apples, never hun–

gry. Boss whip me once for fightin' and I never fought anymore, I tells you.

"My mistress name Miss Sarah. Her was a Hicklin befo' she marry. Their chillun was: Tom, Billie, Dan and Jason, all dead 'cept Marster Jason. De white overseer was Strother Ford. He give de slaves down the country maybe sometimes, so heard them say, but I didn't see him.

"Did us sing? Yes sir. What us sing? One was what I's gwine hist right dis minute and sing wid your lieve. (Here Charley sang, 'Give me dat old time religion'.)

"Us made 'simmon beer sometime and lye soap just 'bout in de same way, hopper was 'rected for dat. 'Simmons was put wid locust; hickory ashes was used to make soap. Every Christmas us got ginger cake and sassafras tea.

"Doctor Scott was de doctor for de slaves. Us niggers was mighty sad when his son Willie's gun went off by accident and kill him in 1868. De Doctor never smile again after dat cumbustion of dat gun. Does you 'member de time Mr. Till Dixon was drowned? He your uncle? 'Twas de fourth of July, I 'member dat day, and a boy Freddie Habbernick was drowned in Catawba in 1903. Dat river take a many soul over dat other shore, I tells you."

S-260-264-N
Project 935
Samuel Addison
Richland County

DAVE WHITE

Ex-Slave 91 Years Old, Congaree, South Carolina
There Was No God But Mossa An' Missus

"My pa name was Nat White who tell me dat I was bo'n about 1842. My ma was name Jane White. My pa use to carry all de votes from McClellanville to Charleston. He come from Tibbin, South Carolina. He also been all 'round de United States. My Ma's Ma bin name Kate. I had sense to know 'em all.

"I know a heap o' sojus had on nice buttons an' had plumes in dere hats. Dey wus singin' an' playin' on a flute dis song, 'I wish I wus in Dixie,' an' dey went in de big house an' broke up ebery thing. Dey say to me, 'you are as free as a frog,' an' dey say to my pa, 'all your chillun are free.' Dey say 'little niggers is free as a frog' an' we holler much.

"I aint nebber do no work, but I kin 'member I use to wear a pant you call chambery. Ma cook a pot o' peas an' weevils wus always on de top. Ma would den turn mush an' clean a place on de floor, she make a paddle an' we eat off de floor. She use to bake ash cake too. I didn' know 'bout no garden, all I know I eat. Dis what dey put on me I wear em. I nebber know nothin' 'bout shoes.

"My master been name Bill Cooper who had a gal an' a son. De gal been name Mary an' de boy Bill like de daddy.

"Tarbin wus a big house, but I aint nebber know de number o' slaves or 'mount o' lan' dat went wid um.

"De slaves had a church name Lazarus an' some went to de white church. Dey had us bar off frum de whites an' we use to look t'rough a glass door. I member when a preacher say, 'honor your missus an' mossa dat your days may be long for dey is your only God.' My Ma tell me when dey use to lick dem she use to sing dis song, 'do pray for me' en ma say w'en de lickin' got too hot she say 'oh God' en mossa say, 'show me dat damn man', den he say, 'I am your only God. My preacher name wus Sabie Mood.

"De slaves couldn't git any news, but dey had to work on Sunday if de week bin bad. W'en it rain dey use to shuck co'n.

"W'en Bill Cooper die he holler to me, 'I'm burnin' up' an' ma say missus say, 'iron me too hot, she meat is red like fire.'

"We use to sing song like dese;

> 'Mary bring de news an' Martha win de prize.
> I mus die an' will die in dat day
> See dat oars like feathers springing'

"I marry Sarah on December 18th. Him de only one I marry an' we had a big weddin' an' plenty o' somethin' to eat. We had fourteen chillun.

"Pa say mossa use to take de fork an' punch holes in dere body w'en he got mad. People always die frum de pisin.

"Dis is all I know I ain't go tell no lie, dat what pa say, I moved here atter de yankees come."

Reference;

Uncle Dave White,
91 years old
Congaree, South Carolina.

United States. Work Projects Administration

S-260-264-N
Project 1885
Laura L. Middleton
Charleston, S.C.

No. Words: 452

DAVE WHITE
An Old Time Negro

Uncle Dave White, one of the waning tribe lives in a simple homestead down a dusty and wind-swept curved country lane on the out skirt of McClenville, forty miles North of Charleston rests the simple shanty of David White, aged Negro, affectionately known to the Negro and white population for many miles around as "uncle Dave".

His quiet unadulterated mode of living and his never changing grateful disposition typifies the true Southern Negro of pre-Civil War days; a race that was commonplace and plentiful at one time, but is now almost extinct, having dwindled in the face of more adequate educational facilities.

His homestead, resembling a barn more than a place to live in. To protect the house against the hazardous affects of imperilling winds, long poles are made to prop the somewhat dilapidated shanty.

A visit to his home, one dark and dreary day in late December, found him as usual in the best of spirits. He welcomed the visitors with a cordiality that would rival the meeting of two long lost friends. The front has no main entrance; the main door is around the back. There are conspicuous displays of many ancient burlap bags, heavy laden, hanging from high rafters, which contained corn and peanuts.

"But why not keep them in your barn, Uncle Dave!" one would ask.

"Well, suh, I keep mah co'n and grain nuts in yuh so mak eye can sta' on 'em," he replies.

A further inspection of the premises revealed other precautions he had taken against the unwelcomed guests; a crude lock on each door and many other precautionary measures convicted, that he was willing to take no unnecessary chances at having his worldly goods stolen.

His age is truly a matter of conjecture. The more you look at him the more uncertain you become. His droopy carriage and shriveled feature betray you at first sight. The first impression will lead one to believe that he is about one hundred years of age, and later it will appear that he is not that old.

We had known "uncle Dave" for a long time; for years it had been a familiar sight to see him trudging the streets of the town with burlap bags thrown across his shoulders containing such household necessities as grits, salt, sugar, etc., and such articles as the house wives would give him out of sheer sympathy. To every friendly greeting he always had the humble response of "Tank Gawd, my eye is open."

He is well known throughout the town. One Sunday night a short time ago, while the services of a white church were in progress, distinguishable sounds of Amen were heard at regular intervals coming from the outside. On investigating they discovered that it was "uncle Dave" reverently enjoying the proceedings. Many times he has been seen outside the same church listening to the services.

SOURCE

Interview with (Mrs.) Minnie Huges, age 43, 179 Spring Street, welfare worker.

United States. Work Projects Administration

Project 1655
Martha S. Pinckney
Charleston, S.C.

FOLKLORE

Approx. 637 words

TENA WHITE
Interview With Ex-Slave

Everybody in the town of Mt. Pleasant, Christ Church Parish (across the Bay from Charleston) knows "Tena White, the washer," "Tena, the cook," "Maum Tena" or "Da Tena, the nurse"—the same individual, accomplished in each art, but best as a nurse.

The house where Tena lives is the second in a row of Negro houses. The writer, calling from the gate, was answered by Tena, a middle-sized woman of neat figure. As the writer ascended the steps a friendly cur wagged itself forward and was promptly reproved by Tena, who placed a chair, the seat of which she wiped carefully with her dress. The piazza was clean and on the floor a black baby slept on a folded cloth, with a pillow under its head. The writer was soon on friendly terms with Maum Tena, and was told: "As soon as my eye set on you, I see you favor the people I know. My people belonged to Mr. William Venning. The plantation was Remley Point. I couldn't zactly member my pa's name. I member when de war come though. Oh dem drum; I nebber hear such a drum in my life! De people like music; dey didn't care nothing bout de Yankees, but dem bands of music! My mother name Molly Williams. My pa dead long before that. All my people dead. I stayin' here with my youngest sister chile—youngest son. He got seven head ob chillun."

"I can do anything—wash or cook—aint no more cook though. Oh yes" and her eyes sparkled, "I know how to cook de turkey, and de ham wid de little brown spots all over de top. Nobody can collec' my soup for me; I first go choose my soup bone. One wid plenty richness. My chile say, 'While my Tena live I wouldn't want nobody else.' But I couldn't take de sponsibility now."

"Maum Tena, how many children did you have?"

"Maggie an Etta an Georgie an Annie, etc., etc." so fast and so many that one couldn't keep up.

"Wait, Maum Tena. How many were there in all—your own children?"

"I nebber had a chile."

"Oh, those were the children you nursed."

"I marry twice. Caesar Robson an Aleck White."

"Did you ever sing spirituals?"

"No, I nebber had time."

"But you sang lullabies to the children."

"Oh, I sing someting to keep de chile quiet."

"Where is your church, Maum Tena?"

"De Methodist Church right here. I know I got for die some day. He keep me distance,[B] but when I look an see my flesh, I tenk de Lord for ebbery year what pass on my head. Taint my goodness, tis His goodness. Nothing but the pureness of heart will see Him."

Tena was shocked and disgusted at the idea of the Lord being a "black man." She said with perfect certainty that he was "no such."

"We all goin to de same Heaven, and there aint no black people there."

The writer asked Tena her age; before she could answer, her great-niece came to the door and said, "She eighty-eight." Tena was indignant. Her eyes flashed. "I aint goin to hab nobody come along puttin down my age what dunno anyting about it. I ought to be as high as nine. Let um be as high as nine."[C]

"If I didn't been round de house wid white people I wouldn't hab dis opportunity today, an dey good to me an gib me nuf to keep my soul an body together. My mother raise me right. When de Yankee come through we been at Remley Point. My Ma took care ob me. She shut me up and she gard me. De Yankee been go in de colored people house, an dey mix all up, an dey do jus what dey want. Dey been brutish.

"De beautiful tureen, stand so high and hab foot so long" lifting her hands, "an all de beautiful ting smash up, an all de meat an ham in de smoke house de stribute um all out to de people, an de dairy broke up, an de horse an de cow kill. Nothin leave. Scatter ebberyting. Nothin leave."

United States. Work Projects Administration

SOURCE: Tena White, Mt. Pleasant, Christ Church Parish, S.C.
Age: Approximately 90.

Project #1655
W.W. Dixon
Winnsboro, S.C.

BILL WILLIAMS
Ex-Slave 82 Years Old.

Bill Williams lives on the Durham place, nine miles east of Winnsboro, S.C., on the warm charity of Mr. Arthur M. Owens, the present owner. He is decrepit and unable to work.

"I was born a slave of old Marster John Durham, on a plantation 'bout five miles east of Blackstock, S.C. My mistress name Margaret. Deir chillun was Miss Cynthia, Marse Johnnie, Marse Willie and Marse Charnel. I forgits de others. Then, when young Marse Johnnie marry Miss Minnie Mobley, my mammy, Kizzie, my daddy, Eph, and me was give to them. Daddy and mammy had four other chillun. They was Eph, Reuben, Winnie and Jordan. Us live in rows of log houses, a path 'twixt de two rows. Us was close to de spring, where us got water and mammy did de white folks washin' every week. I kep' de fires burnin' 'round de pots, so de water would keep boilin'. Dat's 'bout all de work I 'members doin' in slavery time. Daddy was a field hand and ploughed a big red mule, name Esau. How many slaves was dere? More than I could count. In them days I couldn't count up to a hundred. How, then, I gonna kno' how many dere was? You have to ask somebody else. I'll just risk sayin' dere was big and little ones, just a little drove of them dat went to de field in cotton pickin' time, a hollerin' and a singin' glory hallelujah all day long, and pick two bales a day.

"Marse Johnnie and Miss Minnie mighty good marster and mistress to deir slaves. We had good rock chimneys to our houses, plank floors, movable bedsteads, wid good wheat straw ticks, and cotton pillows. Other folks' slaves was complainin' 'bout dirt floors in de houses, boards to sleep on, no ticks, and rags for pillows. Us got flour bread and 'lasses on Sunday, too, I'm here to tell you.

"They sho' fetch dat catechism 'round on Sunday and telled you who made you, what Him make you out of, and what Him make you for. And they say dat from de crown of your head to de top of your big toe, de chief end of every finger and every toe, even to de ends of your two thumbs, was made to glorify de Lord! Missus more 'ticular 'bout dat catechism than de marster. Her grandpa, old Marster John Mobley was a great Baptist. After de crops was laid by, every August, him visit his granddaughter. While dere, he take de slaves and dam up de branch, to make a pond for to pool de water. Then he take to de hill just 'bove, cut down pine tops, and make a brush arbor to hold de prachin' in. 'Vite white preachers, Mr. Cartledge, Mr. Mellichamp or Mr. Van, to come hold a 'vival for all de slaves in and 'round and 'bout de country. I's seen 27 go down and come up out dat pool, a splashin' water from deir faces, one Sunday evenin'. A terrible thing happen one time at de baptism. It was while de war was gwine on. Marse Johnnie had come back from Virginia, on a furlough for ten days. Old Marse John come to see him and fetch Rev. Mr. Cartledge wid him. People was pow'ful consarned 'bout 'ligion 'long 'bout dat time. Me and all de little slave boys jined dat time and dere was a little boy name Ike, a slave of old Doctor John Douglas, dat jined. Him was just 'bout my age, seven or eight years old. After him jined, him wanna back out of goin' down into de water. Dat evenin', after dinner, us was all dressed in a kind of white slip-over gown for de occasion. When it come Ike's time to receive de baptism, him was led by his mammy, by de hand, to de edge of de water and his hand given to de preacher in charge, who received him. Then he commenced: 'On de confession——'. 'Bout dat time little Ike broke loose, run up de bank, and his mammy and all de slaves holler: 'Ketch him! Ketch him!' Old Marse John holler: 'Ketch him!' They ketch little Ike and fetch him back to old Marse John and his mammy. Marse John explain to him dat it better to have water in de nose, now, than fire in de soul forever after. Little Ike say nothin'. His mammy take his hand and lead him to de preacher de same way her did befo'. Little Ike went down into de water. Preacher take him but when little Ike got down under dat water, de preacher lose de hold and bless God, in some way little Ike got 'twixt and 'tween de preacher's legs and comin' out behind him, turnt him sommersets and climb out on de bank a runnin'. Little Ike's mammy cry out: 'Ketch him! Ketch him!' Old marster say: 'No let him go to de devil. Thank de Lord him none of our niggers anyhow. Him just one of Dr. Douglas' Presbyterians niggers dat's destined to hell and be damned, I reckon."

Project #1655
W.W. Dixon
Winnsboro, S.C.

JESSE WILLIAMS

Ex-Slave 83 Years Old.

At the end of one of the silent streets of west Chester, S.C., that prolongs itself into a road leading to the Potter's Field and on to the County Poorhouse, sets a whitewashed frame cottage. It has two rooms, the chimney in the center providing each with a fireplace. A porch, supported by red cedar posts, fronts the road side. In this abode lives Jesse Williams with his daughter, Edna, and her six children. Edna pays the rent, and is a grenadier in the warfare of keeping the wolf from the door.

"You say I looks pretty old? Well, you's right 'bout de old part but I's far 'way from de pretty part. I got a hand glass in my house and when I shaves on Sunday mornin's, I often wonders who I is. I doesn't look lak me. My best friend couldn't say I got much on looks, but my old dog rap his tail on de floor lak he might say so, if him could speak.

"I's been off and on dese streets of Chester for eighty-three years. I was born a slave of Marse Adam C. Walker and my old miss was Mistress Eliza, dat's his wife.

"My pappy name Henry and mammy name Maria. I can see them plowin' in de field right now. Mammy plowin' same as pappy and me runnin' 'long behind, takin' de dirt off de cotton plants where de twister plow turnt de clods on de plants. Then, when dat cotton field git white and red wid blooms in summer and white agin in de fall, I have to shoulder my poke and go to de field and pick dat cotton. I 'members de fust day dat I pick a hundred pounds. Marse Adam pull out a big flat black pocket-book and gived me a shinplaster, and say: 'Jesse, ever time your basket h'ist de beam of de steelyards to 100, you gits a shinplaster.' I make eighty cents dat year but I have to git up when de chickens crow for day and git in de field when de dew was heavy on de cotton. Does I think dat was cheatin'? Oh, no sir! I wasn't 'ceivin' old marster. Him wink at dat, and take a pound off for dew. I'd a made more money but they took me out de field in November, to drive de mules to de hoss-gin. Dat was play work, just a settin' up dere and poppin' de whip.

"Marster live in a big two-story, eight-room house. De kitchen was out from de house. After Christmas, dat year, I was house boy and drive de buggy for Miss Eliza when her want to go visitin'. I was fed well and spent my money for a knife, candy, and firecrackers.

"My marster and missus have chillun. They was Peter, Jerry, Miss Elnora, and Miss Sallie, dat I play wid in slavery time.

"De Yankees didn't come as far up as Chester. They branched off down 'bout Blackstock, took de sunrise side of dat place and march on 'cross Catawba River, at Rocky Mount. I stay on wid Marse Adam and Miss Eliza, after freedom. I marry a handsome gal. Yes, sir, she dark but not too shady. I harks back to them days, as I sets here in dis rocker a talkin' to you. Did I tell you her name? Her name just suit her. Not Jane, Polly, Mag, Sallie, and de lak of dat! Them was too common for her. Her name Catherine, dat just fit her. Us have ten chillun and her and all them 'cept me and three chillun done gone over to Jordan. Dere was just one thing 'bout Catherine dat I's dubious 'bout. She lak to dance, and I was too clumsy for to ever cut a double shuffle. I 'spect I cut a poor figure at de frolics us went to. Does you think burnin' a candle for her would do any good at dis late day? Why I ask you dat? Well, I has heard them say dat white folks does dat sometimes for deir gone-on ones. My daughter, Edna say: 'It might do you good and it could do mama no harm.' I b'longs to Mount Moriah Church in dis very town of Chester. De preacher am Rev. Alexander. He 'low it was superstition to burn dat candle but if I live I's gwine to light one nex' Christmas.

"Us had a good marster and mistress. They was big buckra, never 'sociate wid poor white trash. They wore de red shirt. De time come 'round when they send me to Marse Will Harden and he pass me on to go see Marse Judge Mackey, who live here then. Did I know Judge Mackey? Sho' I did! While he was a settin' up dere on de bench in de court house, he have all de people laughin'. One time de father of Marse W.B. Lindsey beat up a Radical nigger and de case come up befo' him for trial. Great 'citement 'bout it, over de whole county. Court house packed dat day. Solicitor rise and say: 'Please your honor, de 'fendant, Lindsey, put in a plea of guilty.' You might have heard a breast feather of a chicken fall, so very still was de people in dere, though de niggers and 'publicans was a grinning wid joy. Then Judge Mackey 'low: 'Let de 'fendant stand up.' Wid a solemn face and a solemn talk, him wound up wid: 'Derefore, de court sentence you to de State Penitentiary at hard labor for a period of ten years (Then him face light up, as he conclude), or pay a fine of one dollar!' De white folks holler: 'Three cheers for Judge Mackey!' De judge git up and bow, and say: 'Order in de court.' As dere was no quiet to be got, clerk 'journed de court. De judge take his silk beaver hat and gold headed cane and march out, while de baliffs holler: 'Make way! Make way for de honorable judge!' Everybody took up dat cry and keep it up long as de judge was on de streets. Oh, how dat judge twirl his cane, smile, and strut.

"Did I ever see a spirit? 'Spect I has and I sho' have felt one more than once. 'Spect I was born wid a caul over my eyes. When de last quarter of de moon come in de seventh month of a seventh year, is de most time you see spirits. Lyin' out in de moon, befo' daybreak, I's smelt, I's heard, I's seed and I's felt Catherine's spirit in de moon shadows. I come nigh ketchin' hold of her one night, as I wake up a dreamin' 'bout her but befo' I could set up, I hear her pass 'way, through de treetops dat I was layin', dreamin' under.

"Then another time, I was settin' here 'bout four o'clock in de moonlight a lookin' 'cross de street to de town hall. I see sumpin' rise and jump upon dat rock a lyin' dere 'ginst de town hall. It was de figger of a man. Who it was I don't know, though they de call de rock de 'Aaron Burr Rock', 'cause he made a speech standin' on dat rock, long befo' I was born. De people in de library can tell you 'bout dat speech. Maybe Dr. Lathan tell you 'bout it. Him ninety-five years old dis last past twelfth day of May and knows all 'bout de days dat are gone.

"I live wid my daughter, Edna, and I just can make it back dere from de post office every day."

United States. Work Projects Administration

Code: Folk-Lore
Project 1885 -1-
District #4
Spartanburg, S.C.
May 26, 1937

MARY WILLIAMS

Folk-Lore: Ex-Slaves

Aunt Mary Williams stated she remembered slavery times, for she was a girl large enough to walk four miles to go to work "while slavery was on". She said Mr. Alfred Brown used to own her mother, but she was raised by Mrs. Margaret Taylor who used to live where the oil mill is now, below Arkwright Mills. Her father was owned by Mr. Simpson Bobo and drove his horse for him. She stated she was a good hoe-hand, but didn't pick cotton, as Mr. Brown didn't raise any cotton, just raised something to eat.

She said her master was a kind man, didn't allow any "paterollers" on his place, yet she had seen other slaves on other plantations with bloody backs and arms from the whippings they got. When asked why they were whipped, she replied, "Just because their masters could whip them; they owned them and could do what they wanted to them". Her master didn't allow any whipping on his place. One time he kept a slave from another plantation who was fleeing the "paterollers" on his place and in his own house until he was set free.

"I'se got the looking glasses and the thimble my great-grandmother used to use when she worked. She was a good weaver and a good sewer. She made a man an overcoat once, but didn't get but $1.25 for it; she made a pair of men's breeches and got fifty cents for making them. They didn't get nothing for making clothes in those days".

She remembered when the Yankee soldiers came into Spartanburg. She said they took all they could get, stole something to eat, just went into the stores and took liquor and handed it out drink by drink to the other soldiers. Aunt Mary stated she saw Abe Lincoln when he came through Spartanburg; said he was armed himself and had soldiers all around him. He told the colored folks who seemed scared of him that he wasn't going to hurt anybody, not to be scared of him. (Here she must have confused Lincoln with some one else, probably Colonel Palmer, who commanded a detachment in pursuit of Jefferson Davis, which stopped over-night in Spartanburg in April, 1865. FK.)

SOURCE: Aunt Mary Williams, 391 Cudd St., Spartanburg, S.C.
Interviewer: F.S. DuPre, Spartanburg, S.C.

Project 1655
Genevieve W. Chandler
Georgetown County, S.C.

FOLKLORE

WILLIS WILLIAMS
Ex-Slave Story

"When wuz I born? Born in August. When I wuz born been August. I wuz a man grown pulling boxes, (turpentine boxes) when the shake wuz. I know the very night the shake come— — on a Wednesday night. I wuz on door step loosing my shoe string. There wuz more religion then than they is now. Praying and prayer meeting for a month. Everybody tend meeting.

"I been with the Yankee. I kin tell you bout the Yankee. They come home there to Rock Creek when the war wuz breaking up and carried me to Fayetteville. (N.C.) Kept me with 'em till Johnson surrendered in Raleigh,— —then they kept me in Goldsboro and took me on to Petersburg. After everything over they give me free transportation back home. Free on train back to Fayetteville. They had put all the Yankee clothes on me,— —all the blue shirt, blue coat and bumps on the shoulder,—and when they start me home took all the Yankee clothes way from me. Put gray clothes on me and sent me back. I member they took me up in a way-up-yonder building—to Richmond. Couldn't tell you the depth of it. Man on the ground looked like boy.

"The man I belonged to been Mass John A. Williams. (Born on the Cape Fear.) I goes by Mass John name—Williams. His sons been John, James, Charlie, Wallis, William, James. James come home from army sick. Had the mumps; thirty days furlough.

"Member when the Yankees come. Been Sunday morning. Ride up to the gate on horses. Old Boss happened to come out and walk to the lot. I happened to be at gate. They took his watch out his pocket, his pistol—had it girded to him—and took all he whiskey and catch chickens and guinea and take them all. Then they gone in the lot and took two breeding mares and hitch them in wagon and loaded wagon full o' corn. Then they took the two carriage horses and hitched to carriage, and gone to smoke-house, and fill that carriage full of all Mass John sides of meat and ham and shoulders. I been following and watching to see what all they going to take, and a soldier looked at me and say,

"'Come on little Nigger! Wanter go?'

"And I done like another fool! I rode off behind the two brood mares, on the corn, and where they rested that night, I rested right there.

"It was mighty cold up there. I suffered a heap in the cold fore I got back home. They give me a horse,—saddled and bridled,—and a little bayonet gun. Put me on that horse to drive cattle. Tell me to take all I see. Didn't except nobody cattle. Night come put 'em in pasture—put 'em in anybody field—on the oats, rye, wheat.

"Sometimes rain sho fall.—Had to tend that bunch of cattle rain or no rain. Didn't kill one beef and stop! (Kill) FOUR beeves a day. Go out git the hog and kill 'em. Skin 'em. Didn't scald 'em and clean 'em like we do. Just eat the ham. Rest throw way. Gone to Wilmington, Fayetteville, Rookfish and Beaver Creek.

"General Sherman? Has I hear bout him? I SEEN him! He had a big name but he warn't such a big man; he was a little spare made man. I member now when I seed him the last time. He had two matched horses going down to Petersburg. Six guards riding by the side of his turnout. Oh my God, what clothes he had on! He was dressed down in finest uniform.

"When I leave the Yankee they give me $35.00 in money. I been so fool had never seen no green back. Throwed it away eating crackers and peanuts. And I bought some brogan shoes. If I'd a helt on to that, I'd a been some body today.

"I members it was Sunday morning that General Johnson throwed up his hand at Raleigh. Done with the war!

"Before Freedom I have a good enough time. Just lay round the house and wait on my boss. When Freedom come and I did have to get out and work it most kill me!

"After Freedom my mother wash for family to Beaver Creek. And after Freedom my father went to working on shares. Old Maas John called 'em up and tell 'em,

"'You free, Asa. You free, Lewis. You free, Handy. You free, Wash. You can do as you please. You have to fadge for yourself now.'

"Mass John Williams had four hundred slaves. He was a man had the colored people. He didn't work all on his own plantation. He'd hire out his people to work turpentine.——Put 'em out for so much a year. He'd give 'em blanket, suit, coat, pants. First of the year come, Boss would collect wages for all he hire out.

"That there my second wife. You know how a man is. How many wife I had? Two or three. Lemme see! (Looking at present wife) You is one! You the last one! Fust one been Jinny Lind. Next one been Mary Dickson. And Caressa Pyatt been one! And there been another one! I forgot that woman name! Got it in my mouth and can't call it! I'll call the name of them others I take up with in a little while! One was Caline; one was Tissue; (Tisha?) I take them a little while and if they didn't do to suit me, I put 'em out! Some I didn't stay with long nuff to find out they name! Jinny Lind sister was Tissue. Jinny Lind gone, try her sister. Just a 'make out'. If they didn't do to suit me, I'd give 'em the devil and put 'em out.

"Don't know bout beating woman. Some say that bout,

> 'Woman, dog, cypress knee
> more you beat 'em the better they be!'

"But some woman, the more you beat 'em the worse the devil gets in 'em. Get so they won't 'GEE' nor 'HAW'.

"When I was house boy for old Mass John, waiting on white people, that was the best and easiest time I ever had. Ever Satdy drive Mass John to Fayetteville. Ever Satdy they'd think that store belong to me! I'd eat lumps of brown sugar out the barrel, candy, crackers. Did as I please then; NOW do as I kin!

"'Ways of woman and ways of snake deeper than the sea!' I take that to mean— —mighty few can tell by the trail of a snake whether its coming or going— —

"I hear story bout the rabbit and the fox—all them old things—Some times my mind franzy. Been break up too much! Break two ribs to the lumber mill. Jump out a cart one day and run a ten penny nail through my foot. That lay me up two months. Some mean people ketch me up by that tree yonder with a car and that lay me up sixty-five days. They pick me up for dead that time. All that make my mind get franzy sometimes. Come and go—Come and go."

> SOURCE: Uncle Willis Williams. Age, 89 to 90 years old. Conway, S.C. (Horry County).

United States. Work Projects Administration

Project 1885-1
FOLKLORE
Spartanburg Dist. 4
May 25, 1937

Edited by:
Elmer Turnage

EMOLINE WILSON

Stories From Ex-Slaves

"I was a Garmany before I married Calvin Wilson. My father was Henry Garmany, and my mother Sidney Boozer. My husband was in the Confederate army with his master. Dey was near Charleston on de coast. I was slave of Lemuel Lane, of de Dutch Fork. He was killed after de war, some say by some of his young slaves, but we'uns did not know naything about who killed him. We had a good house to live in on Marse Lane's plantation. I used to work around the house and in de fields. My mother was a good seamstress and helped de white folks sew, and she learn't me to sew had help too. We didn't get any money for our work. One time after de war, dey paid me only $5.00 and I quit 'em. My mother hired me out to work for her, and I didn't have any money, still; so I said I better get me a man of my own. Marse Lane was mean to most of us, but good to me. He whipped me once and I deserved it because I wouldn't answer him when he called me. He jes' give me about two licks. He was mean to my mother, but he wouldn't let his white overseer whip us, and wouldn't let de padder-rollers come around. He said he could look-out for his own slaves.

"We didn't learn to read and write, but some of de white folks had learned my mother, and she learned me some.

"Niggers had to go to church at New Hope, de white folks' church, in slavery time and after de war too. We had Saturday afternoons to do what we wanted, and we washed clothes then.

"On Christmas, Marse would give de slaves some good things to eat and send some to dere families. Niggers had frolics at dere houses sometimes on Saturday nights. When I married, I had a good hot supper.

"Children played all de ole games like, play-ball (throwing over the house), marbles and base.

"Some saw ghosts, but I never saw any of dem.

"Old-time cures was peach tree leaves boiled and drunk for fever; wild cherry bark was good for most anything if took at night. I have used it for curing some things. The best cure I know, is turpentine and a little oil mixed. Swallow it and it will fix you up.

"The Yanks went through our place and took two of the best horses we had. One had a tail that reached the ground. Dey stole lots of victuals. I 'member de Ku Klux wid dere long white sheets, and den de Red Coats wid white breeches. Dey would walk or ride, but dey never harmed us.

"I don't know much about Abe Lincoln, but I reckon he was a good man, and Jeff Davis, too. I don't know Booker Washington but heard he was a good man.

"I joined de church because de white folks did. Dey wants to go to heaven and I do too. I think everybody ought to try to do right. I used to think we could make heaven down here, but if we jes' do right, dats all we can do."

Source: Emoline Wilson (90), Newberry, S.C.
Interviewer: G.L. Summer, Newberry, S.C. May 21, 1937.

Project 1885-1
FOLKLORE
Spartanburg Dist. 4
Sept. 22, 1937

Edited by:
Elmer Turnage

EMOLINE WILSON

Stories From Ex-Slaves

"I was born in Newberry County near Cannon's Creek section in the Dutch Fork. I was a slave of Lemuel Lane. He was killed by some slaves just after freedom. They killed him for his money but didn't find any, it was said. When freedom come, my mistress give me some things to eat when we left.

"I can't work much any more; I am old and I can't get about. I live with my son who works when he can find work. We rent a two-room cottage in town.

"I never heard anything about slaves getting 40 acres of land and a mule. None in that section got any. We had to go to work for other people.

"The Ku Klux Klan never bothered us then, and we never had nothing to do with them, nor with politics.

"There was no slaves living in our section who had come from Virginia."

Source: Emoline Wilson (90), Newberry, S.C.
Interviewer: G.L. Summer, Newberry, S.C. 8/10/37
(See ES IV, MS. #13).

Project 1885-1
FOLKLORE
Spartanburg Dist. 4
June 15, 1937

Edited by:
Elmer Turnage

JANE WILSON
Stories From Ex-Slaves

"I am daughter of Billy Robertson and Louisa Robertson; was born about 77 years ago in Newberry, on Marse Job Johnstone's place. My father lived with Judge Job Johnstone as his extra man or servant. He lived in the house with him, slept in his room and waited on him when he became old; and, too, was the driver of his carriage. He drove him to other courthouses to hold court. After the war, my father was janitor at Newberry College, and he was liked by professors, students, and everybody who knew him as 'Uncle Billy'. At commencement, he always made a speech at night on the campus, which the students enjoyed. He told about his travels from Virginia to Newberry before the war. Judge Johnstone never wanted anybody else to be with him when he traveled.

"I belonged to the Avelleigh Presbyterian Church in Newberry, and was christened in the church by the preacher, the Rev. Buist. Colored people were allowed to be members and set in the gallery when they went to church.

"After the war, a colored man named Amos Baxter was killed by the Ku Klux at the old courthouse. My father was on Judge Johnstone's farm a few miles away. He was sent for and came with another colored man to town, and prayed and preached over the body of Baxter. The Ku Klux came to kill my father for doing this, but they never caught him.

"I had to stay home most of the time and help mama keep house. I never worked in the field but once, and the job was so poor they put me back in the house. That was the old Nance place.

"Once I saw a man hung in Newberry. He was a negro named Thompson and killed a white man named Reid. He killed him at a store in Pomaria and burned it over his body. He was hung near the railroad, and a big crowd was there to see it. That was my first time to see a man hung, and I promised God it would be my last. They asked the negro if he had anything to say, and give him five minutes to talk. He was setting on a box smoking; then he got up and said he reckoned his time was over, he was sorry for all the bad things he had done; that he had killed a boy once for 25 cents, and had killed a little girl for 20 cents. He was sorry for his wife and three weeks old baby. His wife saw him hung.

"The Ku Klux wanted to kill any white people who was Republicans. They killed some negroes. A white man named Murtishaw killed Lee Nance, a store keeper. I was a little girl and saw it. Some little children was standing out in front. Murtishaw came up and said he wanted to buy something or pretended he wanted to; then he went up to Nance, pulled his pistol quick and shot him through the throat and head.

"Judge Johnstone's kitchen was away from the house, a brick building. They had large ovens and wide fireplaces in which they cooked.

"My father's favorite horses, when he drove the family, was 'Knox' and 'Calvin', which they kept for many years. When they died the mistress cried awfully about it.

"My husband died at old Mr. Dan Ward's place, on College Hill, where he was living then."

Source: Jane Wilson (77), Newberry, S.C.
Interviewer: G.L. Summer, Newberry, S.C. (6/9/37)

United States. Work Projects Administration

Code No.
Project, 1885-(1)
Prepared by Annie Ruth Davis
Place, Marion, S.C.
Date, June 11, 1937

GENIA WOODBERRY
Ex-Slave, 89 years

"Glad to see yunnah. Who dese udder wid yah? Who yuh? Lawd, I glad to see yunnah. I nu'se aw Miss Susan fust chillun. Ne'er nu'se dem las'uns. Sicily been yo' mamma nu'se. Nu'se Massa Ben Gause child fust en den I nu'se four head uv Miss Susan chillun a'ter she marry Massa Jim Stevenson. Sleep right dere wid dem chillun aw de time. Miss Susan ne'er didn't suckle none uv dem chillun. I tell yunnah dis much, Massa Jim Stevenson was good to aw uv his colored people en Miss Susan wuz good to me. I sho' born right down yonner to Massa Ben Gause plantation. Gade Caesar en Mary Gause wuz my parents. Yas'um, I is glad to see dese chillun cause yuh know whey white folks hab feeling fa yah, it sho' make yuh hab feeling fa dey chillun. I ole now en I can' 'member eve'yt'ing but I ain' ne'er forge' wha' good times dem wuz."

"My Lawd! Yas, my Lawd, de peoples lib well dere to Massa Jim Stevenson plantation. De white folks hab big house dere wid eve'yt'ing 'bout it jes lak uh town. I couldn't tell yunnah how many colored peoples dey hab dere but I know dis, I hear em say dere wuz more den two hundred uv em dat lib in de quarter. Dey house wuz in uh field offen to itself dere on de plantation en wuz strung aw up en down in two long row lak. Dey wuz set up in good libin' den."

"Coase I ain' lib dere in de quarter wid de udder colored peoples a'ter I ge' big 'nough to be nu'se girl, but I know how dey fare dere. My Massa hab uh smoke house full uv meat en uh barn full uv corn aw de time en eve'y Friday a'ternoon aw de colored peoples hadder do wuz to go dere to de big house en ge' dey share uv meat en 'lasses en corn to las' em de whole week. Ne'er hadder worry nuthin 'bout it tall. Dey hab dey gristmill right dere whey dey grind dat corn eve'y week. Yah ain' ne'er see no sech barn en heap uv meat dese days uz dey hab den. Dem hog killin' days wuz big times fa dem plantation peoples. It jes lak I tellin' yunnah my Massa gi'e he colored peoples mos' eve't'ing dey hab en den he 'low eve'y family to hab uh acre uv land uv dey own to plant. Hadder work dat crop in de night. Make light wid fat light'ud stump wha' to see by. Dat crop wha' dey buy dey Sunday clothes wid. Ne'er hadder hunt no clothes but dey Sunday clothes cause dey hab seamstress right dere on de plantation to make aw us udder clothes. Miss Susan larnt Aun' Cynthia en Starrah en Tenna to cut en sew dere to de big house en a'ter dat dey ne'er do nuthin but make de plantation clothes."

"Aw de colored peoples dere to Miss Susan plantation hab dey certain business to go 'bout eve'y day en dey ne'er didn't shirk dat neither. Miss Susan ain' 'low fa no slack way 'round whey she was. Dere been Yaneyki wha' hadder jes wait on Miss Susan; Becky, de house girl; Aun'

Hannah, de one wha' cook in de big house; Aun' Dicey, wha' al'ays clean up de white folks kitchen; en Sanco, de house boy. Den I wuz de nu'se dere fa dem chillun. Ne'er lak it but I ha'e it to do. Hadder stay right dere to de big house aw de time. Miss Susan ne'er wouldn't 'low me take dem chillun 'way offen no whey en eve'ybody hadder be mindful uv wha' dey say 'fore dem chillun too. I 'member dat big ole joggling board dere on de front piazza dat I use'er ge' de chillun to sleep on eve'y evenin'. I be dere singin' one uv dem baby song to de child en it make me hu't lak in me bosom to be wid my ole mammy back up dere in de quarter. Coase I ain' le' nobody know dat. Dere ain' nobody ne'er been no better den Miss Susan wuz to me. It jes lak dis, I wuz jes uh child den en yah know it uh child happiness to be raise up wid dey mammy."

"Den de colored peoples lib mighty peaceful lak dere in de quarter cause dey ne'er hadder worry 'bout how nuthin come. My Massa see dat dey hab decent libin' aw de time en 'bundance uv eve't'ing dey need. Hadder keep 'round 'bout dey premises clean up eve'whey. I tellin' yuh, child, my white folks wuz 'ticular uv dey colored peoples when dey wuz sick. Dey hab big ole me'icine book dat dey take down when one uv dem ge' sick en see could dey find wha' wuz good fa dey ailment. Den Miss Susan'ud send in de woods en ge' wha' it say mix up fa de remedy en make de me'icine right dere to de big house. Miss Susan'ud al'ays doctor de plantation peoples en carry em nice basket uv t'ing eve'y time dey wuz sick. Effen Miss Susan t'ink dey hab mucha co'plaint, den dey'ud send fa de plantation doctor 'bout dere. Annuder t'ing dey ne'er didn't 'low de colored girls to work none tall 'fore dey wuz shape lak uh 'oman cause dey 'fraid dat might strain dey ne'ves."

"Aw de colored peoples wha' ne'er hab no work to do 'bout de big house wuz field hand en dey hadder ge' up at de fust crow uv de cock in de morning en go up to de big house en see wha' dey wan' em to do dat day. Coase dey eat dey break'ast 'fore dey leab de quarter. Effen de sun look lak it wuz gwinna shine, de o'erseer'ud send em in de field to work en dey'ud stay in de field aw day till sun up in de evenin'. Carry dey basket uv victual en pot 'long wid em en cook right dere in de field. Jes put dey peas en bacon in de pot en build up big fire 'bout it close whey dey wuz workin' cause eve'y now en den dey hadder push de fire to de pot. Den some uv de day dey'ud go in de tatoe patch en dig tatoe en roast em in de coals. Effen it wuz uh rainy day, dey ne'er go in de field. Shuck corn dat day. Dat wuz how dey done."

"Aw dem wha' work right dere to de big house al'ays wuz fed from Miss Susan table to de kitchen. Dere wuz Gran'mudder Phoebe who hadder look a'ter eve't'ing 'bout Miss Susan dairy. De plantation peoples'ud bring dey gourd eve'y morning en leab it dere to de dairy fa Gran'mudder Phoebe to hab fill wid clabber fa em to carry home in de evenin'. Den when Gran'mudder Phoebe wuz finish wid aw de churning, she use'er pour wha' clabber wuz left o'er in uh big ole wooden tray under uh tree dere close to de dairy en call aw dem little plantation chillun dere whey she wuz. She gi'e eve'yone uv em uh iron spoon en le' em eat jes uz mucha dat clabber uz dey c'n hold. A'ter dat she clean up eve'yt'ing 'bout de dairy en den she go to de big house en ge' her dinner. Gran'mudder Phoebe say she could set down en eat wid sati'faction den cause she know she wuz t'rough wid wha' been her portion uv work dat day."

"Den dere wuz Patience wha' work to de loom house. She help do aw de weaving fa de plantation. Weave aw t'rough de winter en aw t'rough de summer. She make aw kinder uv pretty streak in de cloth outer de yarn dat dey dye right dere on de plantation wid t'ing dat dey ge' outer de woods lak walnut wha' make brown, en cedar en sweet gum wha' make purple. Den dey make de blue cloth outer dat t'ing dat dey raise right dere on de plantation call indigo. Dere some uv dat indigo dat does grow up dere on de Sand Hills dis day en time but ain' nobody ne'er worry 'bout it no more."

"Jes uh little way from de loom house wuz de shoe house whey Uncle Lon'on hadder make shoe aw de day. I 'member dey is make aw de plantation shoe dere. Make em outer cow hide wha' dey hadder tan fust. Jes put de cow hide in uh trough en kiver it aw o'er wid oak en water en le' it soak till de hair come offen it. Den dey take it outer dat en beat it 'cross uh log hard uz dey c'n till dey ge' it right soft lak. A'ter dat ley out de shoe lak dey wan' it en sew it up wid dem long hair wha' dey ge' outer de hosses neck. Dat jes de way dey make aw we shoe den."

"Minus en Chrissus Gause hab job dere to de gin house. Dey'ud jes put de cotton in dat gin en de seed go one way en de lent go de udder way. Minus hadder feed de gin en dem udder helper hadder hand de cotton. Den Bacchus hadder work de screw dat press de bale togedder. Yunnah chillun ain' ne'er see nuthin lak dat dese days. Dem hosses pull dat t'ing round en round en dat screw ge' tighter en tighter. Turn out pretty uh bale uv cotton us yunnah e'er hear 'bout in no time tall. My Lawd, I 'member dey is hab bale uv cotton pile up aw 'bout dat gin house."

"En dey is hab dey own blacksmith shop dere on de

place down to de place call de big water. Aw dem peoples from plantation aw 'bout come dere fa Fortune to mend dey plow en t'ing lak dat."

"Yas'um, plantation peoples hadder go dere to de Ole Neck Chu'ch eve'y Sunday. I hear em say dat wuz uh Methodist Chu'ch. Aw dem well to do folks hab dey own pew up dere in de front uv de chu'ch wha dey set on eve'y Sunday. Dey seat wuz painted pretty lak uh bedstead en den de poor peoples set in de middle uv de chu'ch in de yellow kind uv seat. Aw de colored peoples hadder set in de blue seat in de back uv de chu'ch. Peoples ne'er rank togedder den lak yah see de peoples rank togedder dese days. Miss Susan Stevenson en Miss Harriett Woodberry en Miss Maggie McWhite wuz de ones wha' pull togedder den. Know dey chillun time dey hit dat chu'ch door. C'n tell em by dey skin. My blessed, chillun, dere wuz sech uh diffe'ence."

"Dat Ole Neck Chu'ch de same chu'ch wha' yunnah see stand two mile up dat road. Dem peoples oughtna hadder move dat chu'ch neither cause it been dere long time 'fore dey come heah. Ain' been right to do dat. Dem wha' put dat chu'ch dere bury right dere in dat cemetery right 'bout whey dey chu'ch wuz en dem udder peoples ain' hab no right to take dey chu'ch 'way a'ter dey been gone."

"De peoples ne'er hab no cars lak dese peoples hab 'bout heah now. My white folks hab carriage en two big ole white hosses wha' to ride to se'vice en whey dey wanna go den. Coase dey ne'er go aw de time lak dese peoples does dis day en time. Lawd, dem hosses could pull dat carriage too. Dey wuz name Selam en Prince. My Massa en Missus hab seat in de back uv de carriage en I hadder set up dere 'tween dem en de driver en nu'se dem chillun. Isaac wuz Miss Susan driver en he hab seat aw uv he own on de front whey he could mind de hosses. My Lawd, I 'member how I did use'er lub to set up dere in Miss Susan carriage."

"Dese peoples dese days don' know nuthin 'bout dem times den. I 'member how dey use'er sell de colored peoples offen to annuder plantation some uv de time. Man come dere to buy my Gran'mudder a'ter Massa Ben Gause die en tell her to open she mouth so he c'n 'xamine her teeth. Say she say, 'I won' do it.' Wanna know effen dey wuz sound 'fore he buy her. Dat de way dey do when dey sell hosses."

"I 'member when dem Yankees come 'bout dere too. Hear Massa Jim Stevenson say dey mus' herry en hide dey va'uables cause de Yankees wuz comin' t'rough dere en sweep em out. Dey bury dey silver en dey gold watch in de graveyard up in de Beech Field. (De Beech Field wuz de place whey de Indian use'er camp long time ago cause de peoples use'er find aw kinder bead en arrow head wha' dey left dere.) Den Miss Susan put trunk full uv her nice t'ing to de colored peoples house. Ain' been 'fraid de Yankees bother em dere. Didn't no Yankees come no whey 'bout dere till a'ter freedom 'clare en den two uv em come dere en stay right dere to de big house. Dey come to 'vide outer de corn. Hab pile uv corn sot aw 'bout de born (barn) dere wid name uv de colored peoples stick 'bout in eve'y pile."

"Yas'um, I 'member dat aw right. Marry in March dere to my pa house. Us ne'er left Massa Jim Stevenson plantation a'ter freedom 'clare. Ne'er wanna hunt no better libin' den we hab dere. My Lawd, dere sho' wuz big doing 'bout dere when I go' hitch up to Joe Woodberry. Pa kill uh shoat en dey bake cake en hab aw kinder ration cook up. I hab pretty dress make outer white swiss muslin wha' I marry in en aw dem peoples wuz dress up dat evenin'. Dat wuz pretty uh sight uz dere e'er wuz when dey ge' to blowing dat cane en knockin' dem stick en dey aw wuz uh jiggin' 'bout."

"Chillun, seem lak aw de good time gone from heah now. Peoples sho' gotta scuffle fa wha' dey hab dis day en time en den effen dey ge' it, dere ain' no sati'faction no whey 'bout it. T'ing ain' gwinna do nobody no good effen dey gotta worry dey head so mucha 'bout whey de next comin' from."

"Good day, honey. Come back 'g'in. Yunnah white en I black, but I lub yuh."

> Source: MOM GENIA WOODBERRY (Eugenia Woodeberry), age
> 89, colored, Britton's Neck, S.C. (Personal interview, June 1937)

Code No.
Project, 1885-(1)
Prepared by Annie Ruth Davis
Place, Marion, S.C.
Date, November 23, 1937

JULIA WOODBERRY
Ex-Slave, Age ____

"Come in, child. Dis ain' nobody talkin to you from behind dat door, but Julia Woodberry. De door unlatch, just turn de handle en come right in here whe' you can warm yourself by de stove. I tell my daughter for her to take de sick child en walk over dere en make Aun' Liney a visit, while I wipe round bout dis stove a little speck. Cose I ain' able to scour none much, but seems like dis old stove does keep everything so nasty up dat I can' let things bout it get too worser. No, child, I tell dese chillun I done seen most all my scourin days, but I think bout I would do this little job for Alexa dis mornin en let her put her mind to dat child. I say, if I able, I loves to wipe up cause it such a satisfaction. It just like dis, dere ain' nothin gwine shine dat floor en make it smell like I want it to, but soap en water. I don' like dese old stoves nohow. I ain' been raise to dem cause when I come up, de olden people didn' think nothin bout puttin no stoves to dey fireplaces. Oh, dey would have dese big old open fireplaces en would have de grandest kind of fires. My Lord, child, dere wouldn' never be no nastiness bout dey fireplace cause de people never didn' burn no coal in dem days. Slavery people been burn dese great big oak logs en dey would make de finest kind of fires, I say. Yes, mam, I been raise up de slavery way en dat howcome I don' want to be noways departin from it."

"Oh, dat was my granddaughter dat had de straw fever. Yes, mam, look like she mendin right smart since she been settin up. De straw fever, dat what I calls it, but I hear people say it de hay fever. De doctor, he just say it de fever, but from de way he give de pills, it point to de straw fever. Cose dat what we termed it, but like I tell you, some calls it de hay fever. I ain' never hear talk of dat kind of fever till dese late years. Yes, mam, she had a little cold en cough some, but not much. You see, when she first took down, she took wid a blindness en a pain in de stomach at de school en couldn' say nothin. De doctor say de fever was bout broke on her den. You see, she had de pain en, I say, dat a sign de misery broke on her. But dat child, she lay dere on dat bed three weeks en she been mighty weak, mighty weak from de fever. No, mam, she ain' have de fever all de time, but dere would come a slow fever dat would rise on her every night en eat up what strength she had caught durin de day. Cose she ain' never been hearty cause she been havin dis fever long bout two years. No, mam, she been test for de T.B.'s in de school dis last year en dey say dat she never had none of dat. Alexa say she gwine let her get dem shots in time next year. All de school chillun took dem last year. Dey tell me dat be to keep diseases down in school. Cose I don' know nothin bout it cause I been raise de slavery way en dat won' de talk den.

"My mother, she was a freeborn woman. She come

from off de sea beach in our own country. Her people was dese Chee Indians en she didn' have no ways like dese other people bout here. Now, I talkin out of her. Ain' talkin out of nobody else, but her. She told me she was born on de sea beach en her parents was Chee Indians. Dat what she told us chillun. Say, when dey stole her en her brother John, dey come dere in dese big old covered wagons en dey stuffed dem way back up in dere en carried dem off. Oh, she say, she was a big girl when dey run her down en caught her. Like I tell you, I talkin out of her. Her en her brother John was out playin one day, near their sea beach home, en first thing dey know, dere come one of dem big old covered wagons dere. Say, dey never know what to think till dey see dis white man gettin down off de wagon en start makin for dem en dey get scared cause dey been learn white man won' no friend. Say, dey broke en run, but de man come right after dem en grabbed dem up wid his hands en stuffed dem way back up in de covered wagon en drove off. She say, she was runnin hard as she could from de man. I remember, I heard my mother speak bout dat she didn' reckon her mother ever knew whe' dey went. She say, dey cried en cried, but dat never do no good. No, mam, de lawyer Phillips stole her. He didn' buy her cause she told me dey brought dem right on to his home en put dem out dere. Her en her brother John were made house servants in de big house en dey went from one to de other in de Phillips' family till after freedom come here. Ma, she say dat she fared good en dey didn' ill treat her no time, but wouldn' never allow dem to get out de family no more durin slavery days. No, mam, she never didn' have no hard time comin up. Cose she had to put de white people chillun to bed at night en den she could go to parties cross Catfish much as she wanted to, but she would have to be back in time to cook dat breakfast next mornin. You see, dey was house servants en dey stayed right dere in de lawyer Phillips' house all de time. Been raise right down dere in dat grove of cedars cross from de jail."

"Well, she didn' say bout dat. No, mam, she didn' have no word bout whe' if she liked de white folks livin or no when she first come dere. You know, when you in Rome, you has to do as Rome do. Reckon dat de way de poor creature took it. No, child, she didn' tell us nothin bout her home no more den dat she was born a Chee Indian. Yes, mam, my blessed old mother told me dat a thousand times."

"My God, my God, child, I couldn' never forget my old mother's face. She bore a round countenance all de time wid dese high cheek bones en straight hair. I talkin out of her now. Yes, mam, can see Ma face dere fore my eyes right now. It de blessed truth, my old mother didn' have no common ways bout her nowhe'. I don' know whe' it true or no, but de people used to say I took after my mother. I recollects, when I would be workin round de white folks, dey would ax me how-come I been have dem kind of way bout me what was different from de other colored people. You know, de Indians, dey got curious ways. My mother, she wouldn' never take a thing from nobody en she was sharp to pick a fight. Yes, mam, she was quick as dat. (Slaps her hands together.) Been fast gettin insulted. Anybody make her mad, she would leave away from dem en dey wouldn' see her no more in a month or two. Hear boss say dat she was quick tempered."

"Well, child, dat bout all I can know to speak bout dis mornin. You see, some days I can get my 'membrance back better den I can on another day. I say, I gwine get my mind fixed up wid a heap to tell you de next time you come here en if you ain' come back, I gwine try en get round dere to your house. God bless you, honey."

Source: Julia Woodberry, Ex-Slave, Age 70-80, Marion, S.C.
Personal interview by Annie R. Davis, Nov., 1937.

United States. Work Projects Administration

Code No.
Project, 1885-(1)
Prepared by Annie Ruth Davis
Place, Marion, S.C.
Date, November 30, 1937

JULIA WOODBERRY

Ex-Slave, Age ____

"Oh, my God a mercy, child, dat been a time when dat shake come here. I tell you, dat been somethin. I sho remember all bout dat cause I been a grown woman de year dat earthquake come here. Yes, mam, I gwine tell it to you just like I experience it. We had all just been get over wid us supper en little things dat night en I had washed Auntie en Mr. Rowell's feet for dem to lie down en dere come such a sketch of clouds from over in dat direction dat I never know what to make of it. Auntie en Mr. Rowell never know what to make of it neither. I remember, I run out to help my sister dat been out to de paddlin block en, honey, you ain' never live to see no black cloud like dat been. I washed a piece through en den I left off en went back in de house en set down by de fire to dry my feet. I set dere awhile en seems like somethin just speak right out de fire, bout dat time, en tell me to move my feet dat I was in bad shape. En, child, it de truth of mercy, dere come a big clog of dirt out dat chimney en drap (drop) right down in de spot whe' my foot was. I run to Auntie en Mr. Rowell to see could dey tell what dat was, but dey been in just as much darkness as I been. I look up en seems like de loft had lowered itself en could hear a roarin for miles en miles bout dere en could hear de people hollerin every which a way. Yes, mam, could hear dem hollerin miles en on top of miles bout dere. My God, dem people was scared to lie down dat night en such a prayin en a shoutin as everybody do dat night, I ain' never see de like fore den. Ain' see de like since den neither. Next mornin, I go to work for de white folks en dey all go off dat mornin en I tell you, I was scared bout to death in dat big house by myself. I remember, I left out de house en been out in de 'tatoe patch grabblin 'tatoes right along en when I raise up, dat thing was comin down dat 'tatoe row just a whirlin en a makin right for me. Yes, mam, I been so scared. I ain' see whe' I is grow a bit since de shake. I tell you, I thought it was de Jedgment. Den we hear dere was gwine be another earthquake, but de people get on dey knees en dey stay on dey knees en it never come here dat time. Dat one was in another state, so dey tell me. I hear talk dat all de earth caved in en you could see de people down dere, but couldn' nobody get dem. Some people say dat been de devil do dat, but I tell dem de devil ain' had no such power. De Lord been de power dat bring dat shake here, I say."

"Oh, Lord, de people sho fared better in dat day en time den dey do dese days. Cose dey didn' have a heap of different kind of trashy things like dey have dese days, but dey had a plenty to eat en a plenty to wear all de time en den everything was better in dem times, too. Now, I speak bout what I know bout. De rations eat better en de cloth wear better, too, in dem days den dey do now. You see, mostly, de people would make dey own provisions at home. White folks would raise abundance of hogs en cows to run all dey big plantation from one year to de other. Wouldn' never clear out of meat no time cause de stock been let loose to run at large in dem days. De most dat dey bought was dey sugar en dey coffee, but dem what was industrious en smart, dey made most dey victuals at home. Made dey own rice en winnowed it right dere home. Oh, dey had one of dese pestle en mortar to beat it out. Yes, mam, de pestle been big at one end an little at de other end. Den dey would raise turkeys en geese en chickens en dere wasn' no end to de birds en squirrels en rabbits en fish in dat day en time. Dat is, dem what cared for demselves, dey had all dem things. Cose dere was some den like dere be now dat been too lazy to work en dey hand was empty all de time. I remember, dem poor-buckras would just go bout from one house to another en catch somethin here, dere en yonder."

"Den de people never wore none of dese kind of clothes like de people wear dese days neither. When a person got a dress den, dey made it demselves en dey made dey own underskirts den, too. You see, all dese underskirts en bloomers like de people does buy dese days, dey didn' have nothin like dat den. Used to put 10 yard in a dress en 10 yards in a underskirt en would tuck dem clean up to dey waist. En, child, when dey would iron dat dress, it would stand up in de floor just like dere been somebody in it. When I say iron, I talkin bout de people would iron den, too. Yes, mam, when I come along, de people been take time to iron dey garments right. Oh, dey clothes would be just as slick as glass. Won' a wrinkle nowhe' bout dem. Another thing, dey used to have dese dove colored linen dusters dat dey would wear over dey dress when dey would ride to church. Den when dey went in de church, dey would pull dem off en put dem on again when dey started home. Dey was made sort of like a coat suit, except dey was a little fuller en would come clean down to de tail of de dress. You see, dey was meant to protect de dress while dey was gwine along de road."

"De world sho gwine worser dese days, honey. Oh, Lord, de people worser. Yes, mam, dey worser, I say. Dey ain' got de mother wit. Dey weaker en dey wiser, I say, but dey ain' got de mother wit. Can' set down en talk to de people dese days en dey take dat what you got to say in like dey used to. En de people don' take de time to teach de chillun to know good things like dey used to en dat how-come dey have more time to get in so much of devilment dese days. Yes, mam, de people used to have more chillun en dey raised dem, too. Chillun know more den grown people do dese days, I say. People used to know how to carry demselves en take care of demselves more den dey do now. Seems like, de people more rattlin en brazen den what dey used to be."

Source: Julia Woodberry, colored, Marion, S.C.—Age, 70-80.
Personal interview by Annie Ruth Davis, Nov., 1937.

Code No.
Project, 1885-(1)
Prepared by Annie Ruth Davis
Place, Marion, S.C.
Date, November 5, 1937

JULIA WOODBERRY
Ex-Slave, Age ____

"Well, I can speak bout what I used to hear my auntie en my mammy en my grandmammy talk bout what happen in dey day, but I never didn' live in slavery time. My mammy, she been broke her leg long time fore freedom come here en I remember she tell me often times, say, 'Julia, you didn' lack much of comin here a slavery child.' Honey, I mean she been in de family way right sharp fore freedom come here.

"My mammy, she was raise right down dere to de other side de jail to de 'Cedars'. You know dere whe' all dem cedars round dat house what bout to fall down. She belong to de lawyer Phillips dere en he wouldn' never allow her to get out de family. She had been a free woman fore he had stole her off de sea beach to be his house woman. Yes, mam, stole my mammy en uncle John, too, off de sea beach, but uncle John went back after freedom come here. My mammy, she been raise from just a child to be de house woman dere to de lawyer Phillips en she never didn' know nothin bout choppin cotton till her last baby been bout knee high.

"I remember how my mammy used to tell me bout dat de colored people won' allowed to go from one plantation to another widout dey had a 'mit (permit) from dey Massa. Yes, mam, all de niggers had to have dat strip somewhat bout dem to keep from gettin a beatin. Couldn' leave dey home widout showin dat 'mit from dey Massa. You see, de nigger men would want to go to see dey wives en dey would have to get a 'mit from dey Massa to visit dem. Cose dey wouldn' live together cause dey wives would be here, dere en yonder. It been like dis, sometimes de white folks would sell de wife of one of dey niggers way from dey husband en den another time, dey would sell de husband way from dey wife. Yes, mam, white folks had dese guard, call patroller, all bout de country to catch en whip dem niggers dat been prowl bout widout dat strip from dey Massa. I remember I hear talk dey say, 'Patroller, Patroller, let nigger pass.' Dey would say dat if de nigger had de strip wid dem en if dey didn' have it, dey say, 'Patroller, Patroller, cut nigger slash.'"

"Child, I tell you dat been a day to speak bout. When I come along, de women never vote, white nor colored, en it been years since I see a colored person vote, but I remember dey been gwine to vote in dat day en time just like dey was gwine to a show. Oh, honey, de road would be full of dem. Dey had to vote. Remember, way back dere, everybody would be singin en a dancin when dey had de election:

> 'Hancock ride de big gray horse,
> Hampton ride de mule,
> Hancocks got elected,

Buckras all turn fool.
Bow-hoo, oo-hoo, oo-hoo.
Buggety, buggety, buggety etc.'"

"White en black was all in a row dere dancin all night long. Ain' made no exception."

"I hear talk dat when freedom come here, de niggers was just turn loose to make dey livin de best way dey could. Say dat some of de white folks give dey niggers somethin to go on en some of dem didn' spare dem nothin. Dey tell me old Sherman didn' come through dis section of de country, but he sent somebody to divide out de things like so much corn en so much meat to de colored people. Now, I talkin bout dat what I hear de old people say. Put everything in Ben Thompson hand to deal out de colored people share to dem. Yes, mam, he was de one had de chair. Talk bout Sherman give Ben Thompson de chair, sayin what I hear de old people say. I don' know exactly how it was, it been so long since de old people talk wid me. Dat it, it been so long till God knows, I forgot."

"Well, I used to know a heap of dem songs dat I hear my auntie en my grandmammy sing dere home when I was comin up. Let me see, child, dey was natural born song too.

'I got somethin to tell you,
Bow-hoo, oo-hoo, oo-hoo.
I got somethin to tell you,
Bow-hoo, oo-hoo, oo-hoo.
In a bow-hoo, oo-oo-hoo.

Way cross de ocean,
'Mongst all dem nation,
Massa Jesus promise me,

> He gwine come by en by,
> He gwine come by en by.
>
> Dere many miles round me,
> De curried be so bold,
> To think dat her son, Jesus,
> Could write widout a pen,
> Could write widout a pen.
>
> De very next blessin dat Mary had,
> She had de blessin of two,
> To think dat her son, Jesus,
> Could bring de crooked to straight,
> Could bring de crooked to straight.'"

"Dat was my auntie's grandmother Eve piece way back yonder in slavery time. Dat was her piece."

"It just like I tellin you, dat been a day to speak bout. I remember when dey used to spin en weave all de cloth right dere home. Yes, mam, I wore many a wove dress to church. Dey would get dis here indigo en all kind of old bark out de woods en boil it in de pot wid de yarn en make de prettiest kind of colors. Den dey would take dat colored yarn en weave all kind of pretty streaks in de cloth. Dey would know just as good how many yards of dat thread it would take to make so much of cloth."

"Yes, mam, I know dere been better livin long time ago den dere be now. Know it cause I didn' never have no worryations no time when I was comin up. My God, child, I couldn' make a support today if I know my neck had to be hung on de gallows. No, mam, dis here a sin cussed world de people livin in dis day en time."

Source: Julia Woodberry, colored, Marion, S.C.
Personal interview by Annie Ruth Davis, October-November, 1937.

United States. Work Projects Administration

Code No.
Project, 1885-(1)
Prepared by Annie Ruth Davis
Place, Marion, S.C.
Date, November 16, 1937

JULIA WOODBERRY

Ex-Slave, Age ____

"No, mam, I ain' thought bout nothin no more to tell you. Death been in de family en seems like I just been so worried up wid my daughter sick in de house dere wid de straw fever. De doctor, he say it de fever en dat all we know, but it acts like de straw fever all up en down. I tell dem chillun dere de other night dat I would have to go back en get my mind fixed up wid somethin to speak bout fore you come here another time. Yes, mam, have to get my mind together somewhe' or another."

"I been born down dere in Britton's Neck, but most my days was lived up to Mr. Jim Brown's place to Centenary. My father, he was name Friday Woodberry en my mother, she come from off de sea beach in slavery time, so she told me. Say dat her old Massa stole her en her brother John, too, from off de sea beach. When freedom come here, her brother John went back to de sea beach, but my mother say dat she won' in no shape to go back. She went from family to family till after freedom was declared en her white folks wouldn' never have her ill-treated neither en wouldn' never let nobody else have her no time. When she was let loose from de white people, she went to Britton's Neck wid a colored woman. You see, she was a stranger to de country bout dere fore freedom come en she been know dat woman en dat how-come she went wid her. I mean she didn' know de people bout dere cause de white folks didn' allow dey colored people to go bout much in slavery time. Couldn' go nowhe' widout dey had a ticket wid dem. She stayed dere in Britton's Neck till Pa died en den she come back up here to Marion to live, but her white people was scattered all bout den."

"No, mam, I ain' never marry cause you had to court on de sly in dat day en time. I tell you, I come through de devil day when I come along. I was learned to work by de old, old slavery way en, honey, I say dat I just as soon been come through slavery day as to come under a tight taskmassa dat was colored. Yes, mam, if I never did a thing right, my dress was over my head en I was whipped right dere. I was engaged by letter, but dey kept me under dey foot so close till I never didn' slip de hay. I remember, I was stayin dere wid Mary Jane Rowell en she kept me cowed down so worser, I never couldn' do nothin."

"I tell you, I been a grown girl dere when I leave Mary Jane Rowell's house en go to cookin en a washin for Miss (Mrs.) Louise Brown. Yes, child, I love Miss Louise Brown to dis very day cause she been just like a mother to me. Yes, mam, Miss Brown was just as good to me as she could be. Mr. Jim Brown, he give me a house dere on his plantation to live in just to do de house work to de big house, but seems like de other colored people on de plantation would be tryin to down me most all de time cause I was workin ahead of dem. I know I would go dere to work many a mornin cryin, from what dem niggers been mouthin bout me, en Miss Brown would cry right along wid me. I tell you, Miss Brown was a tender hearted woman, so to speak bout. I tell Miss Brown, 'Carolina say I stole a towel off de line.' En Miss Brown say, 'Julia, if dere a towel gone off dat line, I know whe' it gone.' No, child, I ain' never think bout to lay no shame on dese hands. White folks been used to leave money all bout whe' I bresh (brush) en dust en I ain' never had no mind to touch it no time. Yes, mam, I been through a day since I come here. Erelong I move out Mary Jane Rowell's house, I been in white people house. If it ain' one class, it another. De very day dat Dr. Dibble been pronounce me to de hospital, dey come after me to wait on a woman. Yes, mam, Julia Woodberry ain' beat de state no time. Oh, I tell you, it de God truth, I has done every kind of work in my life. Me en my three chillun dere run a farm just like a man. Why, honey, you ain' know I had three girls? Yes, mam, dem chillun been born en bred right dere in de country to Centenary."

"I hear people talkin bout dat thing call conjurin, but I don' know what to say dat is. It somethin I don' believe in. Don' never take up no time wid dat cause it de devil's work. Dat de olden talk en I don' think nothin bout dat. Don' want nobody round me dat believes in it neither. Don' believe in it. Don' believe in it cause dat en God spirit don' go together. I hear talk dat been belong to de devil, but I was so small, I couldn' realize much what to think cause dat what you hear in dem days, you better been hear passin. No, mam, dey knock chillun down in dat day en time dat dey see standin up lookin in dey eyes to hear. I has heard people say dat dey could see spirits, but I don' put no mind to dat no time. I believe dat just a imagination cause when God get ready to take you out dis world, you is gone en you gone forever, I say. Don' believe in no hereafter neither cause dey say I been born wid veil over my face en if anybody could see spirits, I ought to could. I know I has stayed in houses dat people say was hanted plenty times en I got to see my first hant yet. Yes, mam, I do believe in de Bible. If I hadn' believed in de Bible, I wouldn' been saved. Dere obliged to be a hereafter accordin to de Bible. Dere obliged to be a hereafter, I say. I can' read, but I talkin what I hear de people say. Dat a infidel what don' believe dere a hereafter."

"How-come I know all dat, I was raise up wid de old people. Come along right behind de old race en I would be dere listenin widout no ears en seein widout no eyes. Yes, mam, I took what I hear in, lady, en I ain' been just now come here. I been here a time. Dat de reason I done wid de world. God knows I is done. I is done. I recollects, way back yonder, Pa would sing:

> 'Dey ain' had no eyes for to see,
> Dey ain' had no teeth for to eat,
> En dey had to let de corncake go,
> Gwine whe' all de good niggers go.'"

"Dat was my father's piece dat he used to sing in slavery time. Dat right cause I can remember back more so den I can forward."

Source: Julia Woodberry, colored, age—about 70 to 75., Marion, S.C.
Personal interview by Annie Ruth Davis, Nov., 1937.

Project 1885 -1-
District #4
Spartanburg, S.C.
June 1, 1937

Edited by:
E. Fronde Kennedy

GEORGE WOODS
Folk-Lore: Ex-Slaves

While looking for an ex-slave in a certain part of Spartanburg this morning, I was directed across the street to "an old man who lives there". I knocked at the door but received no answer. Then I noticed an old man walking around by the side of the house. He was tall and straight, standing about 6 feet 2 inches. He said that his name was George Wood and that he was 78 years of age.

He stated that he was born during slavery, and lived on Peter Sepah's place in York County. Peter Sepah's farm, where he was born, was near the North Carolina line; it consisted of approximately 200 acres. His parents were named Dan and Sarah Wood. His mother was given to old man Sepah by his father as a wedding present, and his grandfather had been given to an older Sepah by his parent as a wedding present. He said it was the custom in slavery times that a slave be given to the son or daughter by the white people when they got married.

He was too young to work, but about the time the war was over, he was allowed to drive the horses that pulled the thrasher of wheat. His master used to walk around and around while the wheat was being thrashed, and see that everybody was doing their work all right. His father lived on another plantation. There was only one family of slaves on the whole plantation. He, his mother, and five children lived in a one-room log cabin about 30 or 40 feet from the "big house". Their beds consisted of straw mattresses. They had plenty to eat, having the same food that the white folks did. They ate ash cakes mostly for bread, but once a week they had biscuits to eat. When the wheat was thrashed, they had biscuits mostly for breakfast; but as the wheat got scarcer they did not have much wheat to eat. He said that Buffalo Creek flowed pretty close to their place and that the creek emptied into Broad River. Shelby, N.C., their market, was about ten miles distant. He thinks that it was easier then than now to get something to eat.

The log cabin where he and his mother lived was kept comfortably warm in the winter time. All they had to do, was to go to the wood-pile and get all the wood they needed for the fire. His mother worked on the farm, washed clothes and helped with the cooking at his master's house. The slaves stopped work every Saturday afternoon about three o'clock; then his mistress would have his mother to patch their clothes, as she did not like to see their clothes needing patching. "We used to have lots of fun," he said, "more than the children do now. As children, we used to play marbles around the house; but no other special game."

Uncle George said that the patrollers saw that the colored people were in their houses at 8 o'clock every night. "They would come to the house and look in; of course, if a man had a pass to another plantation or some place, that was all right; or if he had some business somewhere. But everybody had to be in the house by 8 o'clock." He also stated that if a slave strayed off the plantation and didn't have a pass, if he could out-run the "pateroller" and get back upon his own place, then he was all right. The only slave he ever saw get a whipping, was one who had stayed out after hours; then a switch was used on him by a "pateroller". He said he never saw any slaves in chains or treated badly, for his master was a good man, and so was his "Missus". One day his mother went to a church that was not her own church. On coming back, she saw a "pateroller" coming behind her. She began to run, and he did too; but as he caught up with her, she stepped over a fence on her master's place and dared the "pateroller" to do anything to her. He didn't do a thing and would not get over the fence where she was, as he would have been on somebody's place besides his own.

He said that when the corn-shucking time came, both whites and blacks would gather at a certain plantation. Everybody shucked corn, and they all had a good time. When the last ear of corn was shucked, the owner of the plantation would begin to run from the place and all would run after him. When they caught him, he was placed on the shoulders of two men and carried around and around the house, all singing and laughing and having a good time. Then they would carry the man into his house, pull off his hat and throw it into the fire; place him in a chair; comb his head; cross his knees for him and leave him alone. They would not let him raise a second crop under his old hat—he had to have a new hat for a new crop. Then they would all, colored and white, gather to eat. The owner of the farm would furnish plenty to eat; sometimes he would have some whiskey to drink, but not often, "as that was a dangerous thing to have".

He said that if a man who was chewing or smoking met a woman, he would throw his tobacco away before talking with the woman.

There was plenty of fruit in those days, so brandy was made and put into barrels in the smoke-house; and the same way they had plenty of corn, and would put up a still and put the whiskey they made into barrels.

People in those days, he said, had "manners". The white and colored folks would have their separate sections in the church where they sat. "I've seen a white man make another white man get up in church and give his place to a colored man when the church was crowded." He said his father was baptized by Rev. Dixon, father of Tom Dixon, who was a Baptist preacher. His mother was sprinkled by a Methodist white preacher, but he was baptized by a colored preacher.

Asked about marriages among the slaves, he said the ceremony was performed by some "jack-legged" colored preacher who pronounced a few words and said they were man and wife.

He said the colored people did not know much about Jeff Davis or Abraham Lincoln except what they heard about them. All that he remembered was a song that his Missus used to sing:

> "Jeff Davis rides a big gray horse,
> Lincoln rides a mule;

> Jeff Davis is a fine old man,
> And Lincoln is a fool."

Another song was:

> "I'll lay $10 down and number them one by one,
> As sure as we do fight 'em,
> The Yankees will run."

One day his "Missus" came to their house and told his mother they were free and could go anywhere they wanted to, but she hoped they would stay on that year and help them make a crop. He said his mother just folded her hands and put her head down and "studied". She decided to stay on that year. The next year, they moved to another plantation, where they stayed for twenty years.

"Before they were free, every colored man took the name of his master, but afterwards, I took my father's name."

He said that the Yankee soldiers did not come to their place, but they were ready for them if they had come. The silver was buried out in the lot, and stable manure was piled and thrown all about the spot. The two good horses were taken off and hidden, but the old horse his master owned was left. He said that sometimes a Confederate soldier would come by riding an old horse, and would want to trade horses with his master. Sometimes his master would trade, for he thought his horse would be taken anyway. His master would never get anything "to boot", as the soldier didn't have the "to boot" when the trade was made. So the soldier would ride off the horse, leaving the poor, broken-down one behind. Sometimes after the war, the Confederate soldiers would come by the house, sick, wounded and almost starved; but his mistress would fix something to eat for them; then they would go on.

"'Possum and 'taters were plentiful then. When a slave wanted to go hunting, he could go; but we had to work then—nobody works now." He said that on rainy days, his mother did not have to go to the field, but stayed at home and sewed or carded. He said that after freedom came to the slaves, he worked on a farm for $5.00 a month. After he had been on the farm for many years, he heard that Spartanburg was on a boom, so he came here and worked at railroading for many more years. He has quit work now; but still does a little gardening for some white folks. He said that the white people in the South understand the colored people.

When asked if he had ever seen a ghost, he replied that he had never seen one and had never seen a person who had. "I don't believe in those things anyhow," he said. He also stated he had never heard of anybody being "conjured" either. He said that all the niggers in his section were scared of the niggers from way down in South Carolina, for their reputation as conjurers was against them, so they always fought shy of them and didn't have anything to do with the "niggers from way down in South Carolina".

SOURCE: George Woods, 337 N. View St., Spartanburg, S.C.
Interviewer: F.S. DuPre, Spartanburg, S.C.

Project #1655
W.W. Dixon
Winnsboro, S.C.

ALECK WOODWARD

Ex-Slave—83 Years.

"You knows de Simonton place, Mr. Wood? Well, dats just where I was born back yonder befo' de war, a slave of old Marster Johnnie Simonton. Five miles sorter south sunset side of Woodward Station where you was born, ain't it so? My pappy was Ike Woodward, but him just call 'Ike' time of slavery, and my mammy was name Dinah. My brother Charlie up north, if he ain't dead, Ike lives in Asheville, North Carolina. Two sisters: Ollie, her marry an Aiken, last counts, and she and her family in Charlotte, North Carolina; sister Mattie marry a Wilson nigger, but I don't know where they is.

"Us lived in a four-room log house, 'bout sixteen all told. Dere was pappy and mammy (now you count them) gran'pappy, Henry Davis, Gran'mammy Kisana, Aunt Anna, and her seven chillun, and me, and my two brothers and two sisters. How many make dat? Seventeen? Well, dat's de number piled in dere at night in de beds and on de floors. They was scandlous beds; my God, just think of my grands, old as I is now, tryin' to sleep on them hard beds and other folks piled 'scriminately all over de log floors! My Gran'pappy Henry was de carpenter, and old marster tell him 'if you make your beds hard, Henry, 'member you folks got to sleep on them.'

"I was just a little black feller, running 'round most of de time in my shirt tail, but I recollect pickin' cotton, and piddling 'round de woodpile, fetchin' in wood for white house and chips and kindling to fresh up de fires. Us had plenty to eat, 'cause us killed thirty-five hogs at a time, and de sausages and lights us did was a sight. Then de lard us made, and de cracklin' bread, why, I hungers for de sight of them things right now. Us niggers didn't get white flour bread, but de cracklin' bread was called on our place, 'de sweet savor of life.'

"Money? Us had eyes to see and ears to hear, but us just hear 'bout it, never even seen money.

"My marster had a fish pond, signs of it dere yet.

"My white folks attended church at Concord Presbyterian Church. Us went dere too, and us set up in de gallery. Yes, they asked us. De preacher asked us to jine in some of de hymns, especially 'De Dyin' Thief' and 'De Fountain Filled Wid Blood,' and dat one 'bout 'Mazing Grace How Sweet de Sound Dat Save a Wretch Like us.'

"Our young Marster Charlie went off to de war, got killed at Second Bull Run. Marster Watt went and got a leg shot off somewheres. Marster Jim went and got killed, Johnnie too, Marster Robert was not old enough to carry a gun.

"De young mistresses was Mary and Martha. Marster John, old mistress and all of them mighty good to us, especially when Christmas come and then at times of sickness. They send for de doctor and set up wid you, such tendin' to make you love them. When de Yanks come us all plead for Marster John and family, and de house not to be burnt. De house big, had ten rooms, big plantation, run fifteen plows.

"You ask 'bout was dere any poor white folks 'round? Not many, but I 'members old Miss Sallie Carlisle weaved and teached de slaves how it was done. Marster give her a house to live in, and a garden spot on de place, good woman. She show me how to spin and make ball thread, little as I was. Marster John had over fifty slaves, and they worked hard, sun up to sun down. It's a wonder but I never got a whippin'.

"Did I ever see a ghost? Mr. Wood, I seen sumpin' once mighty strange, I was gwine to see a gal Nannie, on de widow Mobley place, and had to pass 'tween two graveyards, de white and de colored. She was de daughter of Rev. Richard Cook. When I was just 'bout de end of de white graveyard, I saw two spirits dressed in white. I run all de way to de gal's house and sob when I got dere. I laid my head in her lap and told her 'bout de spirits and how they scared me. I still weepin' wid fear, and she console me, rub my forehead and soothed me. When I got quiet, I asked her some day to be my wife, and dat's de gal dat come to be years after, my wife. Us walk to church hand and hand ever afterwards, and one day Preacher Morris, white man, made us husband and wife. I 'members de song de white folks sung dat day. 'Hark from de tomb a doleful sound'. Don't you think dat a wrong song to sing on a weddin' day? 'Joy to de World,' was in our heart and dat tune would have been more 'propriate, seems to me.

"Marster John give de slaves every other Saturday after dinner in busy seasons, and every Saturday evening all other weeks. Us had two doctors, Doctor Brice at first, and when he git old, us had Doctor Lurkin.

"Was glad when marster called us up and told us we was free. De Yankees made a camp on de Doctor Brice place, and foraged de country all 'round. They made me run after chickens and I had to give up my onliest blue hen dat I had. My pappy was took off by them to Raleigh, wid dat I 'member, was de saddest day of slavery time.

"Nannie and me, under de providence of de Lord Jehovah, has had three chillun to live, and they have chillun too. I owns my own home and land enough to live on, though it is hard to make both ends meet some years.

"How I got my name, you ask dat? Well, after freedom us niggers had to come to Winnsboro and register. Us talk 'bout it by de fireside what us would lak. When us come, Marster Henry Gaillard had a big crowd of Gaillard niggers 'bout him beggin' for names. One of them say, 'Marster Henry, I don't want no little name, I wants big soundin' name.' Marster Henry write on de paper, then he read: 'Your name is Mendozah J. Fernandez, hope dats big enough for you.' De little nigger dwarf seem powerful pleased and stepped to de register. De rest of us spoke to Captain Gaillard and he said no better name than Woodward, so us took dat name. Its been a kind of a 'tection to us at times, and none of our immediate family has ever dragged it in a jail or chaingang, Bless God! and I hope us never will."

Project #1655
W.W. Dixon
Winnsboro, S.C.

MARY WOODWARD

Ex-Slave 83 Years Old.

"I knows you since you 'bout dis high (indicating). When was it? Where I see you? I see you at your auntie's house. Dat was your auntie, Miss Roxie Mobley, other side of Blackstock. You was in a little dress dat day, look lak a gal. Oh! Lordy, dat been a long time! What us has come thru since dat day and de days befo' dat, beyond freedom.

"I was born a slave of old Marster Adam Berber, near de Catawba River side de county, in 1854. I's a mighty small gal but I 'members when pappy got his leg broke at de gin-house dat day, in de Christmas week. Seem lak dat was de best Christmas I ever had. White folks comin' and a gwine, loadin' de bed down wid presents for pappy and mammy and me.

"What my pappy name? He was name Joe and mammy go by Millie. Both b'long to Marster Adam and Miss Nellie. Dat was her name and a lovely mistress she be in dat part of de country. Her was sure pretty, walk pretty, and act pretty. 'Bout all I had to do in slavery time was to comb her hair, lace her corset, pull de hem over her hoop and say, 'You is served, mistress!' Her lak them little words at de last.

"They have no chillun and dat was a grief to her more than to Marster Adam. Him comfort her many times 'bout it and 'low it was his fault. Then they 'spute 'bout it. Dats all de rumpus ever was 'twixt them. I 'spects if they had had chillun they wouldn't have been so good to me. What you reckon? They give me dolls and laugh at de way I name them, talk to them and dress them up.

"When de Yankees come, I was a settin' in de swing in de front yard. They ride right up and say: 'Where your mistress?' I say: 'I don't know.' They say: 'You is lyin'. Give her a few lashes and us'll find out.' Another say: 'No, us come to free niggers, not to whip them.' Then they ask me for to tell them where de best things was hid. I say: 'I don't know sir.' Then they ransack de house, bust open de smoke house, take de meat, hams, shoulders, 'lasses barrel, sugar, and meal, put them in a four-horse wagon, set de house, gin-house and barn afire and go on toward Rocky Mount. Our neighbors then, was Marster Aaron Powell and Sikes Gladden, on Dutchman Creek.

"After freedom I marry Alf Woodward. Us had chillun. How many? Let me see; Eli still alive, don't know where he is though. Rosa dead; Susannah live now on Miss Sara Lord's place, up dere near Metford. De rest of de chillun went off to Arkansas 'bout 1885, and us never heard from them.

"I forgot to tell you dat when de Yankees come and find me a settin' in dat swing, I had on a string of beads dat Miss Nellie give to me. Them rascals took my beads off my neck, and what you reckon they did wid them?

Well, if you doesn't know, I does. De scamps, dat is one of them did, took my lovely beads and put them 'round his horse's neck and ride off wid them, leavin' me sobbin' my life out in dat swing. They say you must love your enemies and pray for them dat spitefully use you but I never have pray for dat Yankee scamp to dis day. Although I's Scotch Irish African 'Sociate Reform Presbyterian, de spirit have never moved me to pray for de horse and rider dat went off wid my beads dat my mistress give me. When I tell Marster William Woodward, my husband's old marster, 'bout it, him say: 'De low dirty skunk, de Lord'll take vengeance on him.' Marster William give Alf a half a dollar and tell him to git me another string of beads, though Alf never done so.

"Alf was Marster William's coachman and him and Wade Pichett, dat was a slave of Marster William, took fifteen mules, when de Yankees come, and carried them in de Wateree swamps and stayed dere and saved them. Every time Alf or Wade see Marster William, as de years comed and goed, they fetched up de subject of them mules and git sumpin' from him. One day he laugh and say: 'Look here Alf, I done 'bout pay for sixteen mules and dere was but fifteen in de drove.' Alf laugh but he always got way wid it when he see any of de Woodward white folks. Well I's glad to go now, though I has 'joyed bein' wid you. De Lord bless you and keep you."

Project, 1885-(1)
Prepared by Annie Ruth Davis
Place, Marion, S.C.
Date, September 15, 1937

PAULINE WORTH

Ex-Slave, 79 Years

"Yes'um, I know I been here in slavery time, but wasn' large enough to do nothin in dat day en time. I reach 79 de first day of November. To be certain dat how old I is, Miss Betty Evans give me my direct age here de other day. She know who I am cause I was raise near bout in de same yard dat she was raise in. Mr. Telathy Henry family was my white folks. Yes'um, I was raise right here in dis town. Ain' never been nowhere else but Marion."

"I was small den, but I remembers my old Missus. I sho remembers her all right. My old boss, he died. I can' remember nothin much bout dem times only I recollects when my old Missus used to get after me en whip me, I would run under de house. Didn' want to sweep de yard en dat how-come she get after me wid a switch. I was small den en she was tryin to learn me."

"No, child, I didn' live on no plantation. Didn' have no quarter for de slaves dere. My white folks live in town en dey just have my mother en her chillun en another old man. He stayed in de kitchen en would work de garden en go off on errands for de Missus. My mother en we chillun stayed in a little small one room house in de yard en he stayed in de kitchen. I wasn' large enough to do nothin much den only as like I tell you, my old Missus tried to learn me to sweep de yard."

"I was small den, child, but I got along all right cause we ate in de white folks kitchen. Oh, no'um, dey cook in de chimney long bout de time I come up. No'um, didn' see no stoves nowhe' when I come up. I remembers we had greens like collards en bread en potatoes to eat sometimes, but say remember all what we had to eat, I couldn' never think bout to do dat. I just knows dat I remembers old Missus provide good livin for us all de time. Wouldn' let nobody suffer for nothin be dat she know bout it. Old Missus used to give us every speck de clothes we had to wear too dat was made out dis here homemade homespun cloth. You see my mother was de cook dere. Old Massa used to keep dry goods store en de first I know bout it, she get de cloth out de store to make us clothes. Den after de old head died, old Missus commence to buy cloth from somebody in de country cause people weave dey cloth right dere on dey own plantation in dat day en time. Had dese here loom en spinning wheel. I remembers old Missus would take out big bolt of cloth en cut out us garments wid her own hands. Den she would call us dere en make us try dem on en mine wouldn' never be nothin troublesome nowhe' bout it. I remembers I used to hear my Missus, when she be readin de paper speak bout Abraham Lincoln en Jefferson Davis, but I was small den en never paid no much attention to it. Only cared bout my new homespun dress wid de pockets shinin right in de front part. My Lord, child, I been de proudest like of dem pockets."

"I hear de older people say de Yankees come en say de Yankees was here, but I was small den. Dey didn' do nothin bout dere dat I know of. I was small en I didn' know. Didn' hear de older peoples say nothin bout it neither."

"Oh, we went to de white peoples service to dat big Methodist church right up dere in dis town what was tore down long time ago. Walked dere to dat church every Sunday en set up in de gallery. Dat whe' all de slaves had place to sit. De only thing I could remember bout gwine to church dere was what I hear dem say. Dey say, 'I believe in God the Father Almighty, Maker of heaven and earth, etc.' Dat all I remembers bout gwine to church dere. Everything I remembers. Don' know as I could tell you dat, but I hear my mother repeat it so much when she come home en be teachin us our prayer. Den Missus teach us de same thing till we get large enough to learn de Lord's Prayer. No'mam, white folks didn' teach us no learnin in dat day en time. Didn' hear bout no books only dese almanacs. When de white folks throw dem out, dey allow us to pick dem up to play wid. Dat all de books we know bout."

"Lord, child, dat was somethin. Dat was sho a time when dat shake come here. I remembers de ground be shakin en all de people was hollerin. Yes'um, I was scared. Scared of dat noise it was makin cause I didn' know but dat it might been gwine destroy me. I was hollerin en everybody round in de neighborhood was hollerin. Didn' nobody know what to think it was. Well, I tell you I thought it must a been de Jedgment comin. Thought it must a been somethin like dat."

"I don' know nothin bout dat. It just like dis, I heard

people speak bout conjurin, but nobody never has talked to me nothin concernin no conjurin. My mother wouldn' allow nobody to talk dat kind of speech to us. No, I ain' never seen none of dem things people say is ghost. No, ain' seen none dat I remembers. My husband died en I was right in de room wid him en I ain' see a thing. Never thought bout nothin like dat. Thought when dey gone, dey was gone. When I was able to work, I didn' have no time to bother wid dem things. Didn' have no time to take up wid nothin like dat. I de one dat used to cook dere to Miss Eloise Bethea's mamma. Dis here de one dey call Pauline."

"I tell you my old Missus was good to us, child, good to us all de time. Come bout en doctor us herself when we get sick. Wouldn' trust nobody else to give us no medicine. I remember she give us castor oil en little salts for some ailments. Didn' give us nothin more den dat only a little sage or catnip sometimes. Dat what was good for colds."

"I don' know, child. I can' tell which de worser days den or dese times. I know one thing, dey dances now more den dey used to. I don' go bout much, but I can tell you what I hear talk bout. I don' know as de people any worser dese days, but I hear talk bout more dances. Dat bout all. Coase de peoples used to dance bout, but dey didn' have dese dance halls like dey have now. Didn' have none of dem kind of rousin places den. De peoples didn' have chance to dance in dat day en time only as dey have a quiltin en cornshuckin on a night. Den dey just dance bout in old Massa yard en bout de kitchen. Oh, dey have dem quiltin at night en would play en go on in de kitchen. Turn plate en different little things like dat. I don' know how dey do it, but I remembers I hear dem talkin somethin bout turnin plate. Wasn' big enough to explain nothin bout what dey meant. I just knows dey would do dat en try to make some kind of motion like."

"Honey, didn' never hear my parents tell bout no stories. My mother wasn' de kind to bother wid no stories like dat. She tried to always be a Christian en she never would allow us to tarnish us souls wid nothin like dat. She raise us in de way she want us to turn out to be. All dese people bout here livin too fast to pay attention to raisin dey chillun dese days. Just livin too fast to do anything dat be lastin like. Dat how-come dere be so much destructiveness bout dese days."

>Source: Pauline Worth, age 79, ex-slave, Manning St., Marion, S.C.
>Personal interview, Sept., 1937 by Annie Ruth Davis.

Project #-1655
Phoebe Faucette
Hampton County

Folklore

DAPHNEY WRIGHT
106 Year Old Ex-Slave

Just around the bend from the old mill pond on the way to Davis Swimming Pool lives a very old negro woman. Her name is Daphney Wright, though that name has never been heard by those who affectionately know her as "Aunt Affie". She says she is 106 years old. She comes to the door without a cane and greets her guests with accustomed curtsey. She is neatly dressed and still wears a fresh white cap as she did when she worked for the white folks. Save for her wearing glasses and walking slowly, there are no evidences of illness or infirmities. She has a sturdy frame, and a kindly face shows through the wrinkles.

"I been livin' in Beaufort when de war fust (first) break out", she begins. "Mr. Robert Cally was my marsa. Dat wuz in October. De Southern soldiers come through Bluffton on a Wednesday and tell de white folks must get out de way, de Yankees right behind 'em! De summer place been at Bluffton. De plantation wuz ten miles away. After we refugee from Bluffton, we spent de fust night at

Jonesville. From dere we went to Hardeeville. We got here on Saturday evening. You know we had to ride by horses—in wagons an' buggies. Dere weren't no railroads or cars den. Dat why it take so long.

"Mr. Lawrence McKenzie wuz my Missus' child. We stayed wid him awhile, 'til he find us a place. Got us a little house. We stayed four years dere, 'til de war wuz over. Dey sent de young ladies on—on farther up de country, to a safer place. Dey went to Society Hill. My old Missus stay. Sae wuz a old lady. When de Yankees come she died. I wuz right dere wid her when she died. She had been sickly. After de war dey all went back to de old place. I had married up here, so when dey went back I stay on here.

"I been right here when de Yankees come through. I been in my house asittin' before de fire, jes' like I is now.

"One of 'em come up an' say, 'You know who I is?'

"I say, 'No.'

"He say, 'Well, I is come to set you free. You kin stay wid your old owners if you wants to, but dey'll pay you wages.'

"But dey sure did plenty of mischief while dey wuz here. Didn't burn all de houses. Pick out de big handsome house to burn. Burn down Mr. Bill Lawton' house. Mr. Asbury Lawton had a fine house. Dey burn dat. (He Marse Tom Lawton' brother.) Burn Mr. Maner' house. Some had put a poor white woman in de house to keep de place; but it didn't make no difference.

"De soldiers say, 'Dis rich house don't belong to you. We goin' to burn dis house!'

"Dey'd go through de house an' take everything'. Take anythin' they could find. Take from de white, an' take from de colored, too. Take everything out de house! Dey take from my house. Take somethin' to eat. But I didn't have anythin' much in my house. Had a little pork an' a week's supply of rations.

"De white folks would bury de silver. But dey couldn't always find it again. One give her silver to de colored butler to bury but he wuz kill, an' nobody else know where he bury it. It wuz after de war, an' he wuz walkin' down de road, an' Wheeler's Brigade kill him.

"Been years an' years 'fore everythin' could come together again. You know after de war de Confederate money been confiscate. You could be walkin' 'long de road anytime an' pick up a ten dollar bill or a five dollar bill, but it wuzn't no good to you. After de greenback come money flourish again.

"De plantation wuz down on de river. I live dere 'cept for de four years we refugee. Dat been a beautiful place—dere on de water! When de stars would come out dere over de water it wuz a beautiful sight! Sometimes some of us girls would get in a little 'paddle' an' paddle out into de river. We'd be scared to go too far out, but we'd paddle around. Sometimes my father would go out in de night an' catch de fish with a seine. He'd come back with a bushel of fish 'most anytime. Dey were nice big mullets! He'd divide 'em 'round 'mongst de colored folks. An' he'd take some up to de white folks for dere breakfast. My white folks been good white people. I never know no cruel. Dey treat me jes like one of dem. Dey say dey took me when I wuz five years old. An' I stay wid dem 'til freedom. I am 106 years old now.

"Dem people on de water don't eat much meat. Twenty-five cent of bacon will last dem a week. Dey cut de meat into little pieces, an' fry dem into cracklings, den put dat into de fish stew. It surely makes de stew good. When dey kill a hog dey take it to town an' sell it, den use de money for whatever dey want. Dey don't have to cure de pork an' keep it to eat. Dey jes' eat fish. Dey have de mullets, an' de oysters, an' de crabs, an' dese little clams. Dey have oyster-stew. Dey have roast oysters, den de raw oysters. An' dey have dey fried oysters! Dat sure is good. Dey fish from de boat, dey fish from de log, an' dey fish 'long de edge of de water wid a net. When de tide go down you kin walk along an' jes pick up de crab. You could get a bucket full in no time. We'd like to go up an' down an' pick up de pretty shells. I got one here on de mantel now. It ain't sech a big one, but it's a pretty little shell.

"I is always glad to talk 'bout de old times an' de old people. We is livin' in peace now, but still it's hard times. We ought to be thankful though our country ain't in war."

Source: Daphney Wright, Scotia, S.C.

Project 1885-1
Folk Lore
District No. 4.
May 28, 1937.

Edited by:
J.J. Murray.

BILL YOUNG

Stories Of Ex-Slaves

Seated on the front steps of his house, holding a walking cane and talking to another old colored man from Georgia, who was visiting his children living there, the writer found "Uncle" Bill Young. He readily replied that he had lived in slavery days, that he was 83 years old, and he said that he and Sam were talking about old times.

He was owned by Dave Jeter at Santuc, S.C.; though he was just a boy at the time his mother was a slave. He used to mind his "Missus" more than anybody else, as he stayed around the house more than anywhere else. His job, with the other boys, both white and black, was to round up the milk cows late every afternoon. The milk cows had to be brought up, milked and put up for the night; but the other cows and calves used to stay in the woods all night long. Some times they would be a mile away from the house, but the boys would not mind getting them home, for they played so much together as they slowly drove the cows in.

When asked if he got plenty to eat in slavery days, he replied that he had plenty, "a heap more than I get today to eat". As a slave, he said he ate every day that the white folks ate, that he was always treated kindly, and his missus would not let anybody whip him; though he had seen other slaves tied and whipped with a bull-whip. He said he had seen the blood come from some of the slaves as they were whipped across the bare back. He said he had seen the men slaves stand perfectly naked and take a beating. He also said that he never had a whipping and that his "Missus" wouldn't let his own mother whip him. She would say, "Don't tech that boy, as he is my Nigger." She told him one day that he was free, but he stayed right on there with her and worked for wages. He got $6.00 a month, all his rations, and a place to stay.

"Uncle" Bill said there was some humor at times when a slave was to be whipped. His hands and feet tied together, the slave would be laid across a rail fence, feet dangling on one side and head on the other side; then the master would give the slave a push or shove and he would fall heavily on the ground on his head. Not being able to use his feet or his hands, the slave's efforts to catch himself before he hit the ground was something funny. "That was funny to us Niggers looking at it, but not funny to the Nigger tied up so."

He said some Yankee soldiers came by the house at times, but they never bothered anybody on the place. "Of-course they would take something to eat, but they never bothered anybody."

After working for Dave Jeter for many years, he moved up to Jonesville, where he married. He lived in or near Jonesville for about thirty years, then he moved with his son, who was a barber, to Spartanburg, and has been here thirteen years.

"I never knew anything about rent 'til I got here. I always had a house to live in, raised my own feed and got my wood off the place. So when I got to Spartanburg I learned what rent was. I just quit work two years ago when I had high blood pressure; and now I ain't able to work. Do you see that Nigger across the street, going to work somebody's garden? Well, if I didn't have high blood pressure, I'd be just as good to work as him."

"Yes sir, with my peck of meal, my three pounds of meat each week and my $6.00 a month wages, I had more to eat than I gets now."

SOURCE: "Uncle" Bill Young. 202 Young Street, Spartanburg, S.C.
Interviewer: F.S. DuPre, Spartanburg Office, Dist. 4.

United States. Work Projects Administration

Project 1885-1
Folklore
Spartanburg, Dist. 4
Feb. 4, 1938

Edited by:
Elmer Turnage

BOB YOUNG

Stories From Ex-Slaves

"March 15, 1862 is de date I allus takes when folks axes how old is you. Dat's de best, to follow one date, den no argument don't follow.

"Some see'd it powerful hard in slavery, others never see'd it so bad. Dat 'pends on you a lot, den it 'pends on dem dat you stays wid. It still like dat everywhar dat I is been, but I ain't been no further dan Spartanburg gwine north, and to Lyles's Ford gwine south.

"From a wee bitty baby dey teach me to serve. Befo' you serves God you is got to know how to serve man. De Bible speaks of us as servants of de Lawd. Niggers can serve him better dan white folks, kaise dat is all dey does if dey stays whar dey belongs. Young folks and chillun being raised up real biggity like dey is now, dey can't serve nothing, kaise if you can't serve your earthly father, how is you gwine to serve your Heavenly Father?

"De big plantation and house whar Mr. Jimmie Jeter's sons stay is whar I first see'd earthly light. Dat place still look fine, and it look fine den, too. When I was 8 years old I started out in de field, afo' dat I did jes' what all little nigger boys did, nothing but eat and sleep and play and have a big time wid de little white boys. Lots of my playmates, both white and black, done gone on now. Some done gone to de bad place and some done gone to Heaven, jes' ain't no use talking, dat's sho nuff de truth.

"War was raging all 'round Charleston and Columbia when I come in dis world so dey says, Yankees camped in half mile of Santuc. I is heard dat everybody was scared. Has even heard dat I cried when dem Yankees come, but all I knows is jes' what I heard. Folks hears lots and dey tells it, and dat's jes' what I is doing now—jes' telling what dey told me when I got big. If folks didn't never tell nothing no worse, it wouldn't make no difference, but often dey takes devilish notions and tells dat what injures, if anybody believes dem.

"Aunt Phyllis Jeter 'low when dem Yankees got to Santuc, she was a weaving jes' as hard as she could for her white folks. She say dat she started to run, but dem Yankees come in de house and throw'd away her yarn and took her and tied her to a tree. When she hollered, dey whipped her. She say dat dey was drunk, but dey never burn't up nothing in de house. Dey went on singing, and she got me to playing and got up de yarn from de dirt in de yard and cleaned it. De Yankees never bothered us no mo', and dey never stayed in Santuc long.

"Once when I was a big boy I got drunk and pa whipped me so hard I never got drunk no mo' till I was married, and den I jumped on my old lady for fun and she hit me wid a bed slat. Dat knocked me sober and I 'cided de best thing for me to do was let liquor go to de devil. When I was young I allus walked to Union. Dat ain't but ten miles down de railroad. Den I used to walk all over Santuc and down to Herbert in Fish Dam. Now I is drapped most all my walking. De chilluns travels fast in automobiles, but I jes' as lieve walk to Union as to ride in dem things. Wrecks kills you off so quick dat you does not have time to repent.

"Walking never has hurt nobody, and I buys leather and tacks it on my own shoes, and in dat way it don't cost me nothing much. Folks goes so fast in dem automobiles, and half de time dey ain't in no hurry kaise dey ain't gwine to nothing no way. I gits on my shoe in de winter and I walks. When I wants to drap in for a chaw at some friend's house, I does. I sets dar till I gits rested and warm and I goes on. If dey eats, I does too, and when I gits to Union my chillun is done out and gone. Jes' de same, I reaches home at night befo' dem.

"Dey has tales to tell about gitting out of gas, and when I axes whar dey been, dey jes' as apt to say Spartanburg as any whars. As long as dey has a quarter dey is allus gwine to ride and come home broke. If you fools wid automobiles, you is gwine to spend lots of time in jail. I ain't never been in jail and I thinks it is a disgrace. My chillun says dat I is 'old timey' and don't know nothing 'bout living. Jes' de same, I likes slow moving, and takes mine out in walking and gits home at dark or soon atter.

"Dese fast ways don't bother me. Dey makes sassy chilluns. Sassy chilluns dat can't serve deir pa need not think dat dey can ride to de Promise Land in narry automobile dat dey is ever seed. Gwine round in fast circles and never gitting nowhars seems to satisfy dem, so I don't know what is gwine to become of dem."

Source: Bob Young (75) Jonesville, S.C.
Interviewer: Caldwell Sims, Union, S.C. 11/10/37

Transcriber's Note:

This text is mainly written in dialect. As such, the majority of the spelling, grammar, and punctuation irregularities have been preserved, with the exception of a number of typographical errors. A full list of them can be found at the end of the text.

www.ingramcontent.com/pod-product-compliance
Lightning Source LLC
Chambersburg PA
CBHW071650160426
43195CB00012B/1415